MR SUNSET

DR DON JAMES

Above: *Father and son. Harry and Jeff on a west peak at Sunset Beach, 1962.*

Previous page: *Sunset Beach, 1977.*
John Witzig

Opposite: *Jeff and son Ryan, Biarritz Surf Festival, 1994.*
J D Chopin

SUNSET
THE JEFF HAKMAN STORY

PHIL JARRATT

GEN X

IN ASSOCIATION WITH

GPG

Above: Cheater five, South Shore, Hawaii, 1964.

Right: Waimea Bay, 1974.

DEDICATION

I would like to explain that in no way, shape or form am I condoning or promoting the use of drugs. I am a product of the surfing culture of California and Hawaii in the 1960s, a generation of people who experimented with new drugs with almost religious intensity. The youth of today are much better educated about the effects of drug use, and if as much had been known years ago about the disease of addiction and the twelve step program to control it, my wife's brother John and many of my friends might still be alive.

I want to dedicate this book to my partners at Na Pali Quiksilver Europe – Harry, Brigitte and John – for teaching me humility and commitment. To Bob McKnight, Bruce Raymond, Danny Kwock, Alan Green and John Law, sorry for all the hassles and thanks for the numerous chances all of you have given me.

To my parents, Doris and Harry, I want to apologise for all the pain I have put you through. Last, but by no means least, I want to thank my wife Cherie for her unconditional support, without which I'm sure I would not have all that I have today, especially our beautiful children, Ryan and Lea.

Jeff Hakman

Above: *The Hakmans at home in Anglet, France, 1996.*
Right: *Portrait, 1996.*

PROLOGUE

The Glide

It wasn't winter. It may have been late fall, but the weather was sunny and the air temperature was quite mild. I'm sure my father picked the day real carefully because it was perfect for me. The tide was a little bit full and there were four feet peaks at The Cove, which is about as small as it breaks. You know, it was mellow. The new board my Dad had made me was seven feet eleven inches and twenty inches wide. He'd single-glassed it to keep the weight down and it was only fifteen pounds, so I could carry it down the hill by myself.

We paddled out and Dad got me into position just as this set came through, a little bigger than the ones we'd watched. He pushed the nose of my board in the direction of the cliffs and yelled, "Paddle, Jeff! Paddle!" I thrust my arms into the water and the wave picked me up. I got to my feet and suddenly I'm gliding down the face of a green wave. At the bottom I knew enough to lean into the wave, stick that rail into the wall and go.

There I am, trimming along the face, gliding, with the wave breaking right behind me. Just incredible! That's what stays with you forever, that sensation of speed, the effortlessness of the whole thing and the beauty of the glide.

The Slide

My average day I'd wake up and have a blast to get me to work. That's if I hadn't been too greedy the night before. If I had, I'd be running around waking people up, trying to score. Sometimes I'd have to score three times a day and it would take three or more hours out of your day. If you could channel the drive you put into scoring into something creative, you'd be so successful.

At Balboa when I had money in the bank I had a $500 a day habit. One time there's this new dope in from Pakistan, very different and much more powerful than the usual China White. It was late at night, we'd been drinking and my friend's girl has a blast and goes right out. We drag her down the hallway and into the bathroom and splash water on her face, blow air into her lungs, but it's serious. We're about to call the medics when she comes around.

Then my buddy has a blast and he goes out too. Jesus! This is how twisted I am, I'm knocking on my room-mate's door to score some coke to try and bring him around. Then we're dragging the blue body up the hall again, panicking. And behind those bedroom doors, my room-mates have no idea how bad this whole deal has become.

Top: Palos Verdes Cove, 1958.
Above: Bangkok boogie, 1980.

> Every junkie's like a setting sun.
> *Needle and the damage done*
> Neil Young 1971

Jeff at Sunset Beach, 1967.

FOREWORD

Live to surf, surf to live is a simple cliché but it aptly describes the kind of involvement surfers have with surfing, the kind of involvement which has consistently snared people of all kinds, ages, shapes and persuasions to enter into the bottomless depths of total commitment.

When I made my commitment to surfing many years ago when I was in high school, I joined the ranks of Punahou High's hard core surf corps. Punahou, Honolulu's old missionary school, had the highest of academic standards back then in the early 1960s, but its surfing credentials were even more impeccable. Big wave pioneers Peter Cole, Ricky Grigg and Fred Van Dyke were on the teaching staff, Fred Hemmings was the jock of the senior year and James Jones was a junior. But the guy that people were starting to talk about on the North Shore of Oahu was a weedy little kid called Jeff Hakman.

By the time Jeff was fifteen years old, the Hakman family was living on the North Shore and Jeff was already a seasoned big wave veteran with several winters under his belt. Together with his surfing buddy Jock Sutherland, Jeff put in an enormous amount of quality time all over a near-empty North Shore. Talk about kids in a candy store! It's easy to see how both Jeff and Jock were able to build the foundations of their illustrious surfing careers.

Gerry Lopez, Maritxu Darrigrand, snowboarding guru Serge Vitelli and Jeff, Biarritz, 1993.

The surfing community of the North Shore was a tight-knit group of friends, and so small was their number that they always welcomed someone new to surf with. Other surfers came and went, but none enjoyed the same family support system nor the advantage of living just down the street from Sunset or the Pipeline.

Can you imagine coming home from school, checking out the waves at Sunset and having a pioneer like Fred Van Dyke tell you: "It's too big kid, too big for me". And then you paddle out there with your dad anyway, and just before dark you're sitting in an outer lineup of clean eighteen feet northwest horseshoe peaks steaming in with savage intensity, feathering for hundreds of yards before they reach you, and then jacking up before exploding. And finally you take off on one, moving backwards up the sucking face as it picks you up, and then you drop, and drop, and drop again. Totally committed, knowing that you get spat out the end, or you probably die.

When he was seventeen years old Jeff Hakman stunned the entire surfing world by winning the first Duke Kahanomoku Invitational at Sunset Beach. This was the grandfather of modern surfing contests, and when a high school kid beat the giants of the sport at their own game, it had to be either a fluke or the beginning of a legend. Ten years later, as the undisputed master of the big wave professional surfing circuit, Jeff had proved that winning the Duke meet was no fluke.

In the winter of 1995 I had the opportunity to "talk story" with Jeff on the North Shore, and it was like stepping back through the windows of time. One moment we were looking out at the frantic scenes of the "ghetto du surf" of the 1990s, the next our reflections had transported us back to a sleepy little place we called "the country", where the only noise you ever heard was the crowing of roosters and the rumbling of a rising swell.

Jeff's achievements in surfing, in business and in the hurly burly of life are now the stuff of legend, but to me it is the depth of his involvement in the early years that is truly awe-inspiring. Now, in his middle years he has come full cycle, enjoying the balance of a loving family, a business involvement with Quiksilver and a passion for surfing that has never dimmed, no matter what.

When you read this, Jeff and Cherie's first-born, Ryan, will be fourteen years old. The wheel turns, the kid can surf, the legend lives on. Bitchin!

Gerry Lopez
Maui, 1996

Big day at G-Land, September 1996.

AUTHOR'S NOTE & ACKNOWLEDGMENTS

Would it be too silly and sentimental of me to suggest that this book is as much about love and friendship as it is about waves and fun and fear?

I don't think so, because when you take the camaraderie and the spirituality out of the surfing experience, you diminish it to the point where it is like, well, any other sport. Jeff Hakman's first half-century on this planet has been built around the thrill of the glide, the heart-stopping, gut-wrenching, near-indescribable buzz of extreme surfing. And extreme is the operative adjective, often crossing over into other aspects of Jeff's being.

Put simply, Hakman has heard the hiss of the dragon almost as often as he's heard the roar of the crowd. His ups have been very, very up; his downs lower than most of us can possibly imagine. And through this incredible spectrum of life experiences, one thing has remained constant. Jeff has stayed true to his spirit and his friends.

Surfing builds bonds that are hard to break, even though at times Jeff has sorely tested them. But the beauty of a spirit like Hakman's is that its loyalty knows no bounds. Whether he's been on the bones of his ass, in the grip of some personal torment or up there in the giddy heights of surf superstardom, he's always been there for his "buds". And they have responded with an understanding and a passion that matches Jeff's own.

I have known Jeff Hakman in one way since 1966 when the coverage of the first Duke meet came out in *Surfer* magazine and I cut out his contest-winning cheater five sequence and stuck it on my bedroom wall. Ten years later I got to know him for real when he did a "running meal" at a roadhouse in the Victorian countryside and left me in the crapper with a hundred buck bill, an enraged proprietor and the police to deal with. We were casual friends and acquaintances for most of the next 20 years as I kind of floated around the periphery of his international circle of friends. But it's only been in the past couple of years that I have come to understand why Hakman is such a special person.

It's not his awesome surfing ability, not his incredible resilience, not even his unmatched sense of fun. It's the child in Jeff, the delight he takes in things like teaching little kids an old hula song, complete with bum wiggles and hand movements, or sharing a wave with a novice. One day in the course of the many hours of interviews conducted for this book, I asked Jeff how he felt when he had let his friends down badly, and being true friends, they had given him one more chance. He thought deeply about this for some time, and I could almost hear the episodes, the relationships ticking over in his brain. And when he answered, his eyes misted over with emotion. He said: "I thought, gee I'm lucky. I'm so incredibly lucky, so blessed, to be given another chance". Then he looked away hurriedly and focused on something out the window and beyond the line of trees.

Jeff Hakman hasn't quite been spat out the end of the huge, filthy, double-sucking, gnarly barrel of life into the safety of the deeper water of middle age, but he's survived the air-borne drop, a couple of dug rails and a skate over bare and jagged reef to reach a mellower section. And it's wide open up ahead and the blue sky beckons.

Harry Hodge pushed harder than anyone to make this book a reality, and has contributed to it with generosity and feeling at every point along the way. John Witzig designed it and masterminded production with his usual professionalism and creativity.

Many people contributed Hakman stories along the way, but I would particularly like to thank: Cherie Hakman, Harry Hakman, Doris Hakman, Bob McKnight, Peter Cole, Felipe Pomar, Fred Hemmings, Gerry Lopez, Steve Pezman, Paul Neilsen, Bruce Raymond, Alan Green, Phil Grace, Brigitte Darrigrand, Francois Lartigau, Robbie Naish and Dick Brewer.

Many of the photographs came from Jeff's personal archives and, while every effort has been made to track down their creators, I apologise to those whose photography may have been used inadvertently without credit. My thanks to Leroy Grannis, Dr Don James, Steve Wilkings, Jeff Divine and Greg Noll for permission to use their superb work covering almost 40 years of surfing history.

Finally, my thanks to Dominique Taylor for administrative assistance in St Jean de Luz, and to Nola Crosby and Sammi Jarratt for the same in Noosa; to Sandee Hodge in Bidart, Cherie Hakman in Princeville, David and Joan Hill in Los Angeles, and, of course, my wife Jackie for meals, beds, and all kinds of help along the way.

Phil Jarratt
Noosa Heads 1996

Above: *Katie and Robby Naish, Jeff, Phil Grace, Sandee and Harry Hodge in Val d'Isere, April 1996.*

Opposite: *Jeff and Harry Hodge in the Pyrenees, 1996.*

CHAPTER I

Right: Three generations of the Hakman family, Inglewood, California, early 1950s.

Below: Harry with catch, Catalina Island, early 1950s.

The South Bay of Los Angeles was a very different place in 1935 when Walter and Louise Hakman and their young family came out from back east and settled in Inglewood. There were no freeways, no traffic jams, no muggings, no drive-by shootings, and their ten-year-old son Harry could roam free through endless fields of flowers in what is now the dense urban sprawl west of the 405.

"From our place it was two miles of lupins and poppies right to the coast", Harry remembers. "No international airport, just a little bitty airfield where my dad got a job."

Work didn't come a moment too soon for Dutch-born Walter Hakman. As a young sailor he had met and married German-born Louise and given up the sea for a career in the new field of aviation. When the couple migrated to America, Walter had found a position with Fokker in New Jersey, but when the Great Depression hit he lost both his job and the family home. The Hakmans moved briefly to Baltimore in search of work, then joined the dust bowlers in the long trek west to start a new life.

The Southern Pacific train line which brought them to Los Angeles had been opened in 1876, when a nephew of Colonel Sam Houston proudly stoked the coals as the iron horse carried the President of the United States to the newest city in the land. When the Hakmans set up house in Inglewood, they lived right around the corner from that railroad engineer's grand-daughter, but they didn't know it until Harry started dating Doris Hughes in his senior year at Inglewood High.

Harry recalls: "She was just wild! Monday night horse riding lessons, Tuesday night semi-pro softball, Wednesday night marching with the cheerleaders...It was hard to get her to stand still". Doris was a California gal, tall, tanned, athletic and fiercely competitive. Harry was tall too, deceptively strong and kind of mellow. She liked horses, he liked anything with a motor. They both liked fun.

When he graduated from school in 1944, Harry went straight into the army, and from there into flight engineering school. By the time he was ready for service the war was almost over, and he saw out the last few months on mess detail in the Aleutian Islands.

When he got back to Inglewood he asked Doris to marry him, and when her mother forbade it, they climbed onto his motor cycle and rode out across the desert to a chapel in Vegas. They thus started their married life in the way they meant to conduct it, free-spirited and without a hint of compromise. They found a little tract house in Redondo Beach and Harry got a job as a toolmaker at North American Aviation. Later he was promoted to design and drafting of airplane parts.

Doris fell pregnant early in 1948 and gave birth to their first child, Jeffrey Earl, on November 18.

Jeff's earliest memories of the house in Gibson Place at Redondo are not of its interior but of a lawn strewn with motor cycle parts. Harry Hakman's career may have been in aviation, but his heart was in the two-wheeled technology of Indians, Nortons and Triumphs. He loved the freedom of the wind in his hair and the open road ahead, and he soon converted Doris permanently from horseback to bike saddle. After Jeff's sister Jeannine was born in 1950, the Hakmans got twin Triumphs, and mother and father would head off for weekends in the redwoods at Yosemite, an infant child secured to each gas tank. Says Harry: "Whenever we rode through a town with the kids on our bikes we'd get such disapproving looks, but we kinda liked that".

Motor cycles became the family's preferred mode of transport in the 1950s. Jeff and Jeannine would straddle the gas tank for outings to Yosemite.

Jeff recalls: "As I got a little older sometimes my Dad would let me steer and I just loved that. What I didn't like was when you'd been straddling the gas tank for a couple of hours and your legs would be all bowed and it hurt to walk".

One day Harry was tuning his bike in the yard and minding Jeff at the same time. He sat the little boy on the seat in his wet diapers while he adjusted the throttle. Suddenly Jeff let out a howl that scared the hell out of Harry. He looked up and saw that Jeff had his little bootie resting on the exposed spark plug and was feeling the playful buzz of an electric current through his tiny body.

Life was like this for the Hakman kids. Born into the Great Depression and coming of age during the deprivations of the war years, neither Harry nor Doris was prepared to forego the pleasures of early adulthood in the bebop era in order to play out the conventional parental role. Harry was an efficient breadwinner and had a good enough job, and both parents loved their children, but hell, Harry and Doris were fun hogs and their kids would just have to get used to that. Says Jeff: "Throughout his twenties and thirties my Dad was just like a big kid. He wasn't going to stop for anything, so we were kind of like passengers on his trip. But I thank him for it to this day."

If the Hakman kids ever had cause to wonder where their father's wildman streak came from, they had to look no further than Grandma Louise, whom they called "Oma". After the death of her husband Walter, every summer Oma would load up her van with camping gear and take Jeff and Jeannine to Yosemite for two weeks. Every morning she would cook vast quantities of bacon over an open fire, then lead the children off on an all-day hike, singing German drinking songs in a robust contralto.

Both Harry and Doris lived for their leisure and never tired of finding new ways to have fun, and since they lived no more than a dozen blocks from the beach, the ocean was one of their favourite play pens. When Jeff was very small his father got hold of a rubber raft and took it down to Manhattan Beach to launch it. He carefully placed his infant son in the back and paddled out into a four feet surf. When a set approached, Harry spun the raft around and paddled down the face of the wave, hooting with exhilaration, but as he bounced through the soup in a prototype re-entry, he glanced over his shoulder to monitor Jeff's appreciation. No Jeff.

Harry dived in and frantically searched the white water. With great relief he scooped up a handful of spluttering, wheezing son. Years later Jeff asked his father: "When you were doing that, what were you thinking?"

Harry replied: "I was thinking, what am I gonna tell the wife?"

When he was about four, Jeff had a little bicycle with training wheels. Late one afternoon he pedalled to a friend's house in Redondo, lost control of the bike on the steep driveway and caught up his trouser leg in the chain. He lay at the bottom of the drive with the bike on top of him and his trousers caught tight. No one came. It started to get dark, the little boy saw monsters in the shadows, pissed his pants and cried himself to sleep. When he awoke it was dark and his father, his friend's father and a policeman were standing over him looking very relieved.

The next day Harry said: "Why didn't you just take your pants off?" Jeff shrugged.

Harry's great love at the beach in those days was fishing and diving. The Southern Californian coast was still bountiful, and Harry knew no greater joy than to spend a day at Palos Verdes Cove at the southern tip of the South Bay, gathering a gunny sack full of lobster and abalone. Often this was a family day out, and in between missions to the outside ledges with his spear, Harry would teach Jeff to use a snorkel in the shallow tide pools of the cove. Jeff's earliest memories of diving days are of endless walks up the cliffs to the car, and of wondering why his family had to eat freak food instead of hamburgers and hot dogs like normal American families.

When Harry bought a skiff with a twenty-five horsepower outboard, the treasures of the waters around Catalina became accessible. With Jeff and sometimes Doris and Jeannine aboard, he would take off from San Pedro in the dawn mist and reach a place called Bird Rock, just off the island, while the water was still oily smooth and the fish were on the bite. Harry would fill his lungs and then dive thirty or forty feet down and hide in the kelp beds with his six foot speargun at the ready. When a big yellowtail presented itself he would blast it, then sprint-swim for the light to get a much-needed breath. Then he would dive back down and wrestle his catch to the boat.

As he got older Jeff would free-dive down to watch his father bring up the catch, but he never used a gun, and he could never get used to the long trips home in the rising wind, the skiff slicing through the chop, thud-thud-thud, and the bait and the fuel sloshing around at his feet.

But if there was one early childhood experience that might have put Jeff off ocean adventures forever, it was a trip to a peninsula near Guaymas in Mexico. Harry took a two-week vacation with the intention of getting away from it all and living off the sea. Diving buddy and photographer Ron Church was coming along and the idea was to provision in Guaymas, tow Harry's skiff to San Carlos, and then ferry people and supplies another ten miles by sea.

The beach Harry had chosen for a campsite was about as remote as you could get in that part of Mexico, which was pretty remote, the climate was hot and unforgiving and there was no fresh water and very little shade. On the positive side of the ledger, the fishing and diving were said to be good and they had brought enough rice and water to last ten days.

As he was making the last trip across the bay with Doris, Ron Church ploughed the skiff into a nasty shorebreak and flipped it. No one was hurt, but when he and Harry hauled the boat ashore they found the outboard motor clogged with sand and salt. While Doris and the two children lay sweating under the shade of two scraggy palm trees, Harry worked furiously for a day and a half to clear the motor. When it was working again, he said to his family: "Okay, now let's relax and enjoy this place".

For Jeff, the magic had already gone. He remembers: "It seemed to me like we were on the moon. My mom didn't say much but it didn't look like she was enjoying it either. There were mosquitoes and the sand was so hot you couldn't walk on it for most of the day. The fishing wasn't that good either. I think we ate rice for the last few days. I just remember some one saying on the way over, 'If the boat breaks down we're dead.' And the boat broke down."

But the Hakmans survived Guaymas, and when they returned home Harry was already plotting ways to make their lives even more of an adventure.

The camp near Guaymas, Mexico.

CHAPTER 2

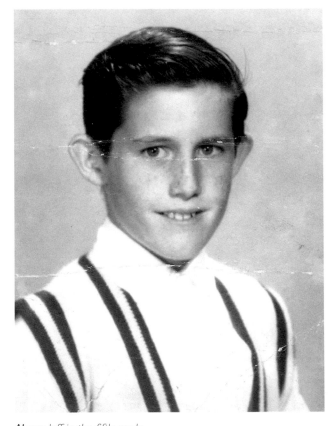

Above: Jeff in the fifth grade.

Above left: Harry Hakman carries his board down to Palos Verdes Cove, 1958.

In 1955 Harry and Doris sold their little home in Redondo Beach and bought upmarket in Via Cadelina in Palos Verdes. In the post-war years the Palos Verdes Peninsula had cemented its reputation as one of the most appealing residential communities in Greater Los Angeles, a place of rugged cliffs, pretty coves and rambling woods. (The name is Spanish for green trees.) It was also fast becoming an enclave for the upwardly-mobile of the Eisenhower years, a place where loyal Americans had flag poles in their front yards and real estate deals were clinched on the back nine of half a dozen different golf courses.

But none of this had any bearing on why the Hakmans moved to Palos Verdes. They were not upwardly mobile and Harry didn't even play golf. In fact the move from Redondo caused them considerable financial hardship, but that didn't matter a damn. They moved because Harry and Doris wanted a better life, and the peninsula, with its clean air and cooling breezes, seemed to offer it. And most importantly, the coves and bays offered the best diving in the entire Los Angeles Basin, and they were right on Harry's doorstep.

Not long after the move to Palos Verdes, Doris gave birth to their third child, Laurie. But the little girl nearly didn't get to celebrate too many birthdays. Harry was working the night shift to allow more time for diving, but he was working seven days to keep up the mortgage payments. One Saturday afternoon, after he'd been barbequing freshly-caught abalone with the family in the backyard, he suddenly realised he was late for work, quickly gathered his things and backed his station wagon out of the garage. He remembers feeling the back right wheel rise up, and then hearing a child scream. He braked, then released and felt the car roll forward again.

The sight of toddler Laurie with tyre tracks right over her upper legs made him sick with fear. He and Doris raced her to hospital where the doctors began the long and painful process of repairing her crushed limbs. She made a full recovery, but Harry has never forgotten the moment. He says: "I can't back up a car to this day without hearing that scream."

Sometime in 1955 the focus of Harry's fascination with the ocean changed from the depths to the surface, where for some years he had noticed with increasing interest the dexterity of the young surfers on their lighter and more manoeuvrable Malibu boards. It was a natural progression anyway, since in those days the Californian waterman tradition was very much alive. If you lived on the coast, you fished, you dived, you surfed, particularly at Palos Verdes. Pioneer surfer Doc Ball had explained the connection in a rousing drinking song he wrote in 1938:

> We hail from Palos Verdes where the
> humpers are the nuts
> We grind the bones of abalone to feed
> our starving guts
> And when they yell "they're humpin',"
> we leap from off our butts
> And slide the soup and ram the rocks and
> jam our feet with cuts.

Harry bought a balsa board from Velzy and Jacobs at Venice Beach and started to surf the mushy summer waves at places like San Onofre and Paddleboard Cove. Doris had ridden a Triumph across the Mojave as fast as Harry, she'd been with him on just about every diving trip, and she wasn't about to be left behind now. She took up surfing too. "But I was never any good", she says today, with just a hint of regret.

As Harry mastered the basics of surfing, he began to look for more powerful waves and found them in the winter surf at Palos Verdes Cove and Lunada Bay. In the summer months Jeff would sometimes venture into the shorebreak white water on his little kickboard, or allow his father to push him on a big board into the small waves as he squealed with delight, but come winter he would sit on the sand or the cliffs and watch Harry go through the arduous ritual of coating himself with baby powder and squeezing into a water-tight rubber diver's suit before paddling way, way out into the lineup.

By 1956 Harry was addicted to California's newest sport and biggest fad. A practical man with creative hands, he began shaping his own surfboards, at first from balsa then later from styrofoam coated with epoxy resin. The garage at Via Cadelina soon became a shaping bay with a carpet of foam dust and the acrid smell of resin rising through the floorboards and filling the house above.

One day Jeff got home from school just as his dad was leaving for work. Harry's face was florid, his hair still wet and sea salt dribbled from the corners of his eyes. "Jeff, Lunada Bay was all time. It was twenty feet, son! Never seen anything like it! Got caught inside, got demolished. Jeff, it was unbelievable. Go take a look at my board." Harry revved the Triumph and was gone. Jeff went into the garage and for a moment didn't see his father's newest board, stacked in pieces on the work bench.

He pestered his mother to drive him down to Lunada Bay before it got dark. When they pulled up overlooking the beach, Doris said: "Your father went out there?" Jeff stared in amazement and horror at the bay full of white water, and somewhere beyond in the gloom, giant waves breaking behind a veil of mist and spray. He thought about the broken board in the garage, the look in his father's red-swollen and salty eyes, and he smiled the thinnest of smiles. He said, "I guess he did. Wow, huh!"

When Jeff was eight years old Harry was flipping through the rack at Velzy and Jacobs, looking for new plan shape ideas to steal, when he happened upon a pig board much shorter than the other boards. He examined it more closely and found it was more or less a scaled down version of the full-sized pig, the wide-hipped, narrow-nosed shape of the moment by shaper-guru Dale Velzy. In fact the board was seven feet eleven inches long and weighed almost thirty pounds, but by the standards of the day it was short, light and totally unorthodox. Harry counted out twenty-five bucks from his NAA pay packet and brought it home for Jeff.

Jeff had only used the board a couple of times (unsuccessfully) at Torrance Beach before

Jeff, front row, third from right, with fellow Little Leaguers.

the mild fall gave way to an early winter and the swell started pumping into Palos Verdes Cove. Harry believed that the stumbling block in Jeff's surfing progression was the fact that he had yet to experience the thrill of gliding across green water, he had been restricted to riding straight in the soup, and he would never know the magic until he had crossed that line and become a real surfer. Thus Harry woke Jeff early on the first Saturday morning with swell in the Cove. Harry led the way down the cliff with Jeff struggling with his heavy board behind. "There's no one out", he yelled. "Perfect."

Father and son paddled towards the lineup as the weather closed in around the cliffs in evil portent. Both felt a knot in the guts at about the same moment, but it was Harry who said, calmly but deliberately: "Okay, Jeff, now paddle hard. Paddle real, real hard".

From Jeff's position the looming eight feet set seemed to block out the sky. His world was suddenly filled with blackness and despair. As he pushed his frail arms and shoulders into overload, he longed to be somewhere warm and dry...and safe. He may have been crying, he couldn't tell. Harry looked over his shoulder and urged him on as they stroked up the face of the first monster. Jeff felt the momentary horror of weightlessness as they pushed through the feathering lip, then slapped down to safety in the trough behind.

Relief lasted all of three seconds. "Paddle hard!" cried Harry, and Jeff sensed the fear in his voice, even over the thunder of the breaking waves. As the wave jacked and started to feather high above him, Jeff heard his father's calls in the distance. He closed his eyes and stroked up the vertical face. He clenched the rails of the little pig as his head smacked into the breaking lip, and he waited for the weightlessness. When it came it was all wrong. The board was being forced back into his face and he was falling, falling into the pit.

Most surfers can remember their first bad wipeout, but most surfers aren't frail and tiny eight-year-olds out in double-overhead surf for the first time. Jeff recalls: "There was this terrible pain in my ears and I knew I was going to drown. Then I kinda popped up and there's another huge wave breaking in front of me. I knew enough to dive deep, then it started all over again."

He washed into the beach, gasping for breath, his lungs filled with the sea, and lay retching and crying until his father arrived. Forty years later, sitting on the deck of his boat in Honolulu's Sand Island marina, Harry Hakman says: "I miscalculated. Badly. I should have watched the sets first, and if I had he never would have been out there. And then when I

On the beach at PVC.

saw that big set coming I should have paddled over and grabbed him. There's a lot of should haves. And when I saw him on the beach like that, I felt so bad, I would not have blamed him if he'd never surfed again."

Never surfing again was exactly what Jeff had in mind. When he had recovered sufficiently to throw a tantrum, he told his father what he could do with the Velzy pig, stomped up the cliff without it and announced he was going back to the Little League. Which he did, playing shortstop (appropriate for someone who was still way short of four feet) for the Cardinals in the minor league. Later he advanced to major Little League with the Indians. He recalls: "I was happy. That was what America was about back then, baseball and hot dogs. Somewhere down the line it turned into football and hamburgers, but by then I didn't care."

As the weeks went by and Jeff showed no inclination to try surfing again, Harry threatened to sell the board. "Damn it, I'll just give it away, Jeff, if you're not even prepared to try."

"So give it away." Eventually Harry did, but in the summer of 1958, he tried again, this time shaping Jeff another seven feet eleven board out of premium female balsa. Harry's shaping had reached a level of expertise where the better surfers of Palos Verdes and Torrance Beach were asking him to build their boards, and the board he built for his son was superbly crafted, a roundtail, twenty inches wide with a near flat bottom, single-coated with fibreglass to keep the weight down to a manageable fifteen pounds.

Jeff couldn't hide his glee when the board was presented to him, but eight months had gone by and he had built a psychological barrier between himself and the surf. One day in the late fall Harry said, "Jeff, it's a beautiful day and there's a neat little wave at the Cove".

"Okay, let's go." Harry couldn't believe the turnaround, but he said not a word as they walked down the cliff and launched into the cool, clear, blue water.

Harry watched from behind and called encouragement as Jeff got to his feet on his first real wave. "That's it, son, nice and easy, swing it around...now go!" Jeff's head disappeared behind the wall as he raced in full trim towards the shoulder, but Harry could see his slight shadow through the back of the wave and knew he was going to make it. Jeff was away now, he was gliding.

The boy fell onto the front of his board as the wave backed into deeper water, and his smile lit a beam to the outside lineup. "All right! Yeah! Did you see that, Dad? Did you see it?"

"I saw it, Jeff. Not bad, now let's get another one."

CHAPTER 3

Right through the winter and into the next spring, Jeff surfed every moment he could. The Cardinals, the Indians, school, chores, nothing else mattered. Harry made him a cutdown dry suit which had to be tied off once he was inside it. The thing chafed like crazy, but it kept him warm and in the waves longer than anyone else.

As the days got longer again, he would race home from school and he and a buddy would tote their boards down to the beach for the last hour of light, one of them carrying noses, the other on tails. At Torrance Beach he hung out with the best of the young surfers, Jimmy Irons, Lonnie Augebright and Dale Streubel, and at Dapple Grey School, back in the riding school and equestrian course belt of the Palos Verdes peninsula, his buddies who surfed were Beith Moore, Jimmy Cardillo, and Billy Grey. Weekdays he hung with the school crew, weekends with the Torrance crew.

The clique of surfers at Torrance was just one of a score or more of surf tribes which had developed along the coast between San Diego and Santa Cruz. There had been outlaw gangs of surfers in California since the 1920s and early 1930s, riding redwood slabs and hollow cigar box paddleboards in the style of their Hawaiian mentors. And in the late 1940s and early 1950s, the technological advances made by surfer designers like Bob Simmons and Dale Velzy had seen the entrenchment of surfer communities at places like Rincon, Malibu and Hermosa.

But by 1958 the scene was starting to go beserk. In the town that had given birth to the concept of Hollywood, it was only a matter of time and production schedules before someone would see the commercial potential of a lifestyle formula which included equal elements of death-defying sports action, anti-social behaviour, narcissism and sick humour. That someone was Frederick Kohner, the father of a young girl who had started hanging out with Tubesteak Tracey, Mickey Dora and the other bad boys at Malibu. He wrote a sanitised comic novel about it which Hollywood rushed onto celluloid as the first of the '50s beach epics, "Gidget". Overnight, the outlaw surf culture was mainstream and hot property.

All right! Go to Hawaii, straight to Hawaii...Ala Moana Park, 1959.

At the same time Hollywood was fast-tracking "Gidget" onto the drive-in circuit, a group of surfers, mostly from the South Bay, were renting high school auditoriums to show their primitive home movies of far-off and exotic surf spots to appreciative and packed houses. While the approved methods of showing appreciation – foot stamping, food throwing, bottle-top snapping and seat ripping – did not exactly endear them to their lessees, surf flick pioneers like Bud Browne, Greg Noll, John Severson and Bruce Brown fuelled the dreams of the surf cultists and convinced them that they had to live life on their own terms, not those of their parents.

The beaches closest to Los Angeles seemed to develop their own elites quicker than anywhere else, and on the South Bay alone, by 1958 there were at least half a dozen crews that kids like Jeff Hakman idolised. By this time big, beefy, no-holds-barred Greg Noll was the top dog in the Manhattan Beach Pier pack, while Dewey Weber and Lance Carson ruled the roost just down the esplanade at Hermosa.

The best surfer and the hero of the Torrance Beach crew was Jimmy Irons' big brother, Ricky, who was smooth, casual, radical and fast all at the same time. Whenever Ricky Irons caught a wave, Jeff and the other kids would stop paddling and watch, but when Lance Carson or Dewey Weber showed up, all the kids would go in and form a rapt gallery on the beach. Jeff recalls: "Dewey Weber was colourful and flashy, like a blaze of colour. He wore bright trunks and his boards always seemed to have bright panels of colour on them. Totally flamboyant, and that was the way he surfed. He'd steer his pig board around one hundred and eighty degrees, then run right to the tip and hang off the nose, then he'd run back with a flourish and launch into a dramatic cutback. Lance Carson was just the opposite. His boards were clear and he'd wear plain black or white trunks. He didn't look anything special until he took off, and then he'd just glide along the face, effortlessly going from one manoeuvre to the next, seamless and flowing. It was like the other guys had a sequence of manoeuvres they had to get through; Lance just stood there and listened to the pulse of the wave."

In 1958 a "surf shop" was still a tiny back room choked with foam dust, shavings and the acrid smell of resin. If you had mentioned to surf shop proprietors like Velzy and Jacobs, Hobie Alter or Gordon "Gordie" Duane the idea that one day such shops might become lifestyle supermarkets, they would have laughed themselves hoarse. But already the surfer style had become a marketable commodity. Jeff and his buddies would not even consider going to the Pier Avenue Auditorium in Hermosa Beach to see "Surf Fever" or "Big Surf" unless they had on regulation attire of Jack Purcell tennis shoes, Levis, Penney's Towncraft tee-shirts and oversized Pendleton shirts over the top. In general, the look was baggy and daggy, much like it is today, and that extended to surf trunks. A tailor in Honolulu named Take made the coolest surf trunks, but they were near impossible to get, and ownership usually implied that you had actually been to big wave Mecca. Like thousands of gremlins along the California coast, Jeff and his buddies made do with boxer shorts, at least four sizes too big and tied with a drawstring.

Early in 1959 a friend of Harry's named Jim Lyman started making surfboards commercially in the South Bay and invited Jeff to become one of his sponsored team riders. Lyman may have seen little more than freak value in having a ten-year-old on his team, but Jeff couldn't believe his luck, getting free surfboards just a matter of months after his first tentative take-off on a real wave.

But his good luck was only starting. Just before Easter break a school friend at Dapple Grey named George Davis told Jeff that he was going to Hawaii for the holidays. "My mom says I can take a friend. Would you like to go?"

"Oh, sure. I'll ask my folks." Jeff maintained his composure until he got round the other side of the lockers. "Yessss!" He punched the air with his clenched fist. "Yes, yes, yes!"

Adele Davis was one of Palos Verdes' better known residents, an internationally acclaimed nutritionist whose several books were considered to be ground-breaking in their field. She had toured and lectured around the world and had extensive social connections in Hawaii, through whom she had arranged for George and his little friend to be accommodated in fine style on Kauai and Oahu. They were to be accompanied by a young governess, but for all intents and purposes they were on their own.

Jeff set off for the airport with his brand-new yellow Jim Lyman eight-feet-six inch double-ender on the roof and his head and heart bursting with anticipation, and maybe just a little fear. He had only one lasting image of the surf in Hawaii, and that was of a horror Waimea wipeout which had flickered onto the screen at the Pier Avenue Auditorium. He tried not to think about that as he and George waved goodbye and boarded the jetliner.

The standard trans-Pacific transport for surfers in those days was a hokey DC-6 prop that left from Burbank and took about fifteen hours, but George and Jeff travelled in style on the newly-introduced 707 jet service, which got them to Honolulu in under five hours.

On Kauai the boys were set up at the Coco Palms Hotel where they discovered good surf right across the street. In between excursions to places like Waimea Falls, they hung out on the beach and surfed the well-formed beach break with just one local, an older boy named Keoke, who taught them how to cook Hawaiian-style in a fire on the sand. Then they moved to Waikiki, staying in a beachfront bungalow at the old Halekulani Hotel.

Says Jeff: "I just couldn't believe my eyes. Kauai had been nice, but this was just paradise. Right behind our bungalow was this central pool and restaurant area where you could eat as much as you wanted at the buffet breakfast. Then around the other side was this big bay full of surf breaks, stretching from Diamond Head back to the airport. I was in heaven. Every morning I'd get up early, wail on that buffet, man, just jam in as much energy food as I could, then paddle my eight-six out there and surf all day. George could surf okay but he wasn't into it the way I was. He'd come in after a couple of hours and go do something else. I'd surf until dark, paddling from one break to the next, from Populars to Canoes, down to Number Threes, over to Queens. Most of the time there was no one even surfing the outer breaks. The water was beautiful and warm, and when the trade winds blew, you could smell the flowers on the water."

When Harry picked him up at the airport he asked, "Well, what was it like?"

Jeff said: "Dad, you gotta go. You just gotta go!"

CHAPTER 4

Christmas 1959, first wave at Makaha.

If Jeff Hakman's life was changed forever by that first experience of the glide at Palos Verdes Cove, his destiny was sealed when he smelled the fragrance of the plumeria flowers across the water in Waikiki.

All summer long he worked hard at improving his surfing through balance, positioning and wave selection. Weight distribution was his only problem area. Heading towards his eleventh birthday, Jeff was, well, puny. In the generations of the Hakman family of which Harry had any knowledge, there had never been a person of less than average build. Indeed, Harry's father had been quite tall and Harry himself was almost six feet, lithe and athletic. Likewise the Hughes clan, and Doris was five-nine in her stockings. Even the little girls were taller than their friends, but Jeff showed no signs of a growth spurt.

"I was actually a little worried that there may have been a birth defect that had affected his legs", Doris Hakman recalls. "But we held off seeing anyone about it, hoping that he would suddenly grow."

Whereas his diminutive build may have held him back in most other sports, Jeff used it to his advantage in surfing. No one could tuck inside a tinier tube, and where most surfers thought brute strength was required, Jeff realised that in duck-diving or eskimo-rolling through a broken wave, timing was everything. In comparison to his body, his arms were solid and long, and from the kneeling position he could plant them deep in the water and sit high and dry on his board and cover an enormous area of water in no time at all.

During the fall and early winter of 1959, Harry drove Jeff up and down the coast in search of the best surf. They liked the powerful waves at Salt Creek, south of Laguna, and often after a surf session, they would sit on the backboard of Harry's station wagon and grill steaks on a portable barbeque.

One midweek evening in November Harry phoned Jeff from his night shift at North American Aviation. "Jeff, there's a big north swell coming up. Rincon is gonna be perfect. We'll leave at four in the morning, so you get to bed right now."

"I can't, Dad. I got a spelling bee at school tomorrow and it's real important."

"Jeff, I'm talking about Rincon here. This is not some, aw gee, I don't feel like going to school deal, this is Rincon, maybe eight feet!"

Jeff missed his spelling bee, Harry phoned in sick and they surfed Rincon all day, six to seven feet and perfect with only local heroes Reynolds Yater and Bob Cooper and three or four other surfers in the water. It was the best surf Jeff had had in his life, all eleven years of it, and he never mentioned the spelling bee to his father again.

Harry says now: "It was wrong to make him come, but it was the physical stuff that drove both Doris and me. We didn't pay enough attention to academic pursuits with our kids, and in some ways I regret that. But this was perfect Rincon, for God's sake!"

Jeff's own memories of 1959 are not just of perfect surf. "It was the year I wished I was just that little bit older, the perfect time in history to be sixteen and a surfer in California. It was light, you know. Nothing heavy. The beach smelled of suntan oil and hamburgers, there weren't too many surfers in the water and there were just enough girls in bikinis on the sand. The Hollywood movies got it pretty right, I think. Life just seemed to revolve around waves, girls, cars, boards and pulling funny pranks on your friends. When I think of 1959 I think of Kundera's 'The Incredible Lightness Of Being', because that was how I felt."

Queens contest, 1960.

Despite absconding from work for a day to surf Rincon, Harry had been working long hours at the plant for months to help clear a backlog of work and put aside some savings. When he was at home, however, he and Jeff talked of nothing but their plans to surf Hawaii together. Doris quietly arranged three weeks' leave for her husband, and on Christmas Day she presented him with two airline tickets to Honolulu. Doris had scrimped and saved to get the money together, so they were booked on the Hokey Airlines DC-6, but it didn't matter, they were going!

After their arrival at Honolulu they checked in overnight at the Halekulani. Jeff explained the lay of the land to his father. "Right, Dad, this is where you get your buffet, the waves are out front."

Harry shook his head. "This is winter, Jeff. The big waves are at Makaha." Jeff looked confused. He had never heard of Makaha.

Harry rented a jeep the next morning and they drove out to the west side and rented a quonset hut at Nanakuli for three dollars a night. The accommodation wasn't quite what Jeff had been accustomed to the previous Easter, but he liked the laidback country feel of Nanakuli, even though it was reputed to be a rough neighbourhood, and from there it was just a short drive to Makaha. The twenty mile coastline was in those days a sparsely populated and tourist-free zone, shunned by many who claimed that the weather was hotter and drier, the roads dustier and the mosquitoes mysteriously worse. But it had a real local feel, with extended families forever staging luaus and playing music on the beaches.

Since 1952 Makaha had been the home of the world's only international surf contest, run under the auspices of Waikiki's Outrigger Canoe Club each December, and it had become the winter home of leading big wave riders like Buzzy Trent and Greg Noll. By 1959 Waimea Bay on the North Shore had been ridden successfully for several seasons, and Sunset Beach was said to be consistently rideable up to fifteen feet or more, but Makaha was still very much big wave headquarters, holding surfable waves in all but the very biggest winter swells. Harry Hakman had heard tales and seen the films of giant Waimea, but as far as he was concerned, Makaha was the place to be.

The main man at Makaha was Richard Keaulana, known as Buffalo because of his mane of unkempt reddish hair. He was the lifeguard and lived in a little house up behind the toilet block. Buffalo made himself known to the Hakmans on their first day at Makaha, after they had come in from a surf session and laid out their towels on the dry sand. He sauntered up to them and said: "Dis not a real good place to leave your stuff. Tide come in, wash dis stuff all away".

The implication was "dumb haoles", but Buffalo had a pleasant, if authoritative manner, and he underlined that authority when he took to the surf. He simply owned the break at Makaha, in any size, any conditions. Jeff recalls: "He was an incredibly beautiful, graceful surfer, and if he fell off, he'd just keep going, bodysurfing. He was a complete natural in the water. The transplanted Californians who lived there, like Buzzy Trent, were really good surfers, but no one had the grace and style of Buffalo at Makaha."

Jeff and Harry got to know the local characters, some of them bad asses with long hair in ponytails (rarely seen in those days) and tattoos. Former champion wrestler Lord Tallyho Blears would come out on the weekends, along with the top Honolulu surfers like George Downing, but the guy who most amused Jeff was George Matsuda, who years later was to become his algebra teacher. George rode a huge balsa board with a plexiglass window cut into the nose and straps on the rails so that he could attach his fishing poles and spears. On the tail he had attached a large fish box to store his bait and the catch. Unless the surf was really good, George preferred to paddle out past the lineup and sit on his board and fish. When he'd had enough he'd paddle in and pick up a wave, manoeuvring the board in and around his luggage.

The surf wasn't particularly good that season, and the only time they tried to take a look at the North Shore, Harry got the jeep bogged on the back road to Kaena Point and they had to turn back, but they'd seen enough to know where the future lay. On the plane ride home, Harry said: "You know, Jeff, we could live there".

"For sure, but what's Mom gonna say?"

"Let's find out."

In fact Doris was quite amenable to the idea, just as she had been to trying out motor cycling, diving and surfing. Harry didn't try to sugar coat it. "There's a lot of wind, you might not like that."

"I can handle wind."

"So you're sure?"

"Sure I'm sure. Let's do it!"

Harry put the Palos Verdes house on the market early in the summer of 1960 and requested a year's leave of absence from North American Aviation, which was given in recognition of his long and valued service to the company, although the request left some of his superiors scratching their heads. The house sold quickly and the family had to move into Oma's house at Inglewood for the last few weeks while Harry and Doris sorted out the final details, and sea-freighted boards, boats, bikes and the other accoutrements of their active lives.

Finally, in the fall they flew out of Los Angeles to start a new life in the sun.

CHAPTER 5

Harry Hakman was thirty-four years old in the fall of 1960, he had a wife and three kids under twelve to support and he had just walked out on the job he had had all his married life, and he had just sold the middle class dream home. There was no certainty of any employment in Hawaii, and certainly nothing in the aircraft industry. Harry had no security and no plans, and he had never been happier in his life.

There was no question about where they would live. They moved straight to Makaha and set up home on the point in rented accommodation that Harry and Jeff remember as a "comfortable little cabin" and Doris remembers as a quonset hut. They were right in the thick of the fishing and surfing community and their close neighbours included Buzzy Trent and his wife Violet.

Doris and the girls took time to acclimatise, but Harry and Jeff fell right into the pattern of local life. With no job and no immediate prospect of finding one, Harry buzzed around the cane fields on his motor cycle and filled his days surfing, fishing and diving. Soon he was trading fish for fresh vegetables from the local market gardens, and the family ate well and cheaply.

Although they couldn't quite see the surf from the house, Harry and Jeff always knew when the swell was up because they could feel it through the floorboards. They would surf together every morning before school, then Harry would swoop Jeff up onto his cycle and buzz him out to school at Waianae, hair and nose still dripping salt water.

While Jeannine and baby Laurie could attend the little local school at Makaha, eighth grader Jeff was enrolled at Waianae High School. The Hakmans didn't know it at the time, but this was reputed to be the worst school on the island, a hotbed of crime and violence. Amongst the true islanders there was, even then, a growing resentment at the way the post-war influx of tourists and new settlers was eroding their traditional way of life. Statehood in 1959 allayed some of the fears about being totally subsumed into the culture of mainland USA, but the resentment still sometimes manifested itself in petty violence

First wave at Sunset on the board Jeff shaped himself.

27

Jeff at Ala Moana with his pride and joy.

against the haoles, particularly when too much swipe (fermented pineapple juice) had been consumed at a luau.

But the haole families who confronted these situations head-on usually found that respect was a two-way street. From the day they arrived the Hakmans adopted an island lifestyle and were treated accordingly. In fact it never even occurred to Jeff that he was one of a handful of haoles in an all-local school. He was immediately accepted by his peers. Jeff recalls: "It helped that by then I was surfing pretty good, and that my Dad rode into school on this hot bike every morning. I was still this little guy from Palos Verdes, of course, but they didn't hold that against me. My only regret was that they all had names like Mongoose or Birdie or something, and I was just plain old Jeff."

Before he left California, Jeff had shaped his first surfboard, under his father's watchful eye. It was a seven feet eleven inch roundtail copied off a Dewey Weber plan shape, and it was perfect for the sometimes-mushy sections at Makaha. The little guy on the little board soon became a fixture in the lineup, and the locals pressured him into entering the Makaha contest in December. Although he didn't progress very far, the word was spreading that the twelve-year-old could handle himself in just about any conditions.

During that winter at Makaha Jeff became friendly with another young surfer named Jackie Eberle, and the two made several sorties to the North Shore to surf Haliewa. Harry also remembers driving Jeff out to the North Shore for some small to medium days at Sunset and Laniakea, but he was still feeling his way. The big guys had only recently started surfing the North Shore with any regularity, and the general concensus was that it was no place for a kid.

By the end of the winter season the Hakman kids had started talking pidgin and were covered with sores they picked up at school. Doris had had enough. She said: "Harry, this might be fine for you but I want a few creature comforts, I want to be near a tennis club and I want the kids in a decent school". Harry had no real objections. Money was running out fast and he needed a job. So they moved into Honolulu, renting a house in mountainside Manoa, a comfortable residential area not far from the centre of town and the surf at Waikiki and Ala Moana. Doris joined a tennis club, Harry went looking for work (and found it, first at a motor cycle shop for a dollar twenty-five an hour, then at a boat shop in Kaneohe for two dollars an hour) and Jeff was enrolled at Stevenson Intermediate High.

In Honolulu, Waianae High was considered to be the worst on Oahu, but Jeff soon found that Stevenson and its neighbour, Roosevelt High in Papakolea, were in a league of their own. Says Jeff: "There were riots in the classroom and guys would steal cars at lunch time. It was heavy, real heavy, and both my parents were concerned about me going there. Fortunately my mom met some people through tennis who were connected with the board of Punahou, and after some intense lobbying over the net, I was accepted for admission."

Established as Oahu College in 1841 by the Reverend Hiram Bingham, Punahou (the Hawaiian name comes from a freshwater spring in the grounds) was intended as a centre for the education of the children of the missionaries. The land on which it was built was a royal bequest from Queen Kaahumanu, who had recently been saved, and no expense was spared on its construction. It was then and remains the finest private school in Hawaii. But if it seemed to Jeff that he had been living out some kind of island-style fantasy at Waianae and Stevenson, and now he was back with the gentility he knew at Dapple Grey, nothing could have been further from the truth. There were strict rules and high standards at Punahou, but it was also the epicentre of the emerging surfing elite, with the hottest surfers on the island either in class or in the staff room.

That summer in town Jeff fell into the Ala Moana scene with consummate ease. The surf spot at the mouth of the Ala Wai Yacht Harbour produced the best and most consistent waves on the South Shore, and its proximity to the major centre of population meant that it was crowded and intensely competitive.

(This situation only got worse as the 1960s wore on, but life was made tolerable in the lineup by strict adherence to the time-honoured island code of rotation, or pecking order. But not everyone understood the importance of the code. At the height of his surfing fame in California, Corky Carroll paddled out at Ala Moana with his name emblazoned all over the top of his red board, started taking waves at random and abusing anyone who got in his way. Finally, one of the locals, Toku, became so enraged that he paddled in, loaded a spear gun and swam back out into the lineup. He popped up alongside Corky and pressed the spear into his stomach. Jeff was watching the action in the water. "Toku was so mad he actually wanted to pull the trigger. You could see it in his eyes. It took all the willpower he could muster not to do it. He just told Corky to paddle in and never come back.")

Donald Takayama was the hottest surfer at Ala Mo from the late 1950s into the 1960s, although by 1961 he was under threat from youngsters like David Nuuhiwa and Tommy Padaka. But Conrad Cunha was the undisputed king. The first rule of surfing Ala Moana was, don't take off in front of Conrad. The second rule was, don't take off in front of anyone else. Built like a Hawaiian king of old, Conrad sat further inside than anyone else, took only the very best set waves and never fell off. He had been surfing Ala Mo longer than anyone cared to remember and he knew the wave inside out.

Says Jeff: "He was extremely polite, never shouted at anyone, always smiling and waving to people to take the wave, he didn't want it. But when his wave came there was no dispute about it. It was Conrad's wave. He might have waited for half an hour, but he'd launch into it, line it up through the bowl from way back and just power through. Nothing could stop him and he was an incredibly gifted, graceful surfer. He was the first surfer I ever saw drive a longboard into an eight feet barrel and come out."

Before the summer was over, Harry wrote to North American Aviation, thanked them kindly and told them he wouldn't be coming back. His family was settled, he had regular work, and he felt ready for the challenge of a North Shore winter. In preparation for the season, both he and Jeff needed new boards.

Through the latter half of the 1950s, the pioneer big wave riders on the North Shore had almost all ridden balsa guns shaped by a reclusive Californian named Pat Curren, but by 1961 there was a buzz about the new guy in town, a former engineer from the Californian boonies called Dick Brewer.

Brewer had opened a little hole-in-the-wall shop in Haleiwa and called it (rather grandly) Surfboards Hawaii. Although he was already in demand to make guns for surfers like Peter Cole and Buzzy Trent, he had heard tales about the weedy little Hakman kid and had seen him surfing Ala Moana during the summer. He had also come to know Harry Hakman in the lineup at Sunset.

Jeff recalls: "I'd been riding a Hobie board and it was a bit of a dog, in fact I was going through the equipment doldrums. Brewer had a keen eye for young kids on the way up and he offered to make me a board for a special price. I was stoked because Brewer was a real character and it was cool to have him making your boards. He liked fast cars and he and Buzzy Trent would get around in this Ford Ranchero, with their Brewer concave guns hanging out the back. They'd pull up at Sunset and as they got out of the car all their empty beer cans would fall out the doors. It was incredibly cool."

Brewer agreed to build Jeff a scaled down conventional malibu for his first full North Shore winter, and in due course Jeff took delivery of a fine-lined seven feet eleven inch "mini-gun". The first Brewer of hundreds.

With the arrival of the first winter swells, Harry and Jeff surfed Haleiwa and Laniakea and small Sunset Point. Finally, during the Christmas vacation, Harry coaxed his son out on a big day at Sunset. The water was unusually glassy and the sets were ten to twelve feet out of the north west. As they paddled out, Harry said: "If you lose your board, don't worry. I'll come and get you". Jeff sat in the lineup with the big wave regulars – Peter Cole, Buzzy Trent, Jose Angel, Fred Van Dyke. There were a few muffled laughs, a few more snide comments. No one had ever seen a kid surf big waves before, and Jeff could feel the pressure. He watched the experts take off on several waves and realised that he didn't have the paddling speed to take off in their lineup. He edged further inside and waited.

When a set wave came, he turned and stroked into it, trying not to think about the consequences. He got to his feet and skated down the steep face, faster, faster. Still driving towards the bottom, he lost control and fell off. Jeff recalls: "I just went plop. I didn't do anything wrong, the board just couldn't handle the size. I thought, okay, now I'm going to die. I had a picture of one of those horrible wipeouts I'd seen in the movies at the Pier Avenue Auditorium, and I just waited for the worst. But somehow I popped out the back okay."

Then he had to face the long and difficult swim. The treacherous channel at Sunset can carry you down the beach and out to sea for miles. The secret is to swim through the white water towards the point, but as this brings you closer to the impact zone, every survival instinct in the novice tells him to do otherwise. Jeff swam into the channel and struggled for half an hour, getting nowhere. Eventually one of the big wave riders paddled past him on the way in.

"Hey, mister, can you help me in?"

"If you can't swim, kid, what the hell are you doin' out here?" The surfer wailed on Jeff for several minutes, then reluctantly put him on the front of his board.

Jeff recalls: "He wouldn't shut up all the way in. I mean, I'd nearly drowned, and he's just in my ear the whole way. Okay, I'd made a mistake, but I think he could have been more compassionate. Strangely enough, I didn't see him much in the lineup after that, and no one else ever gave me a bad time about that wipeout. In fact Peter Cole told me later that he and Buzzy got a huge kick out of seeing me take off on a monster. It was kind of my membership into the club."

CHAPTER 6

Having been smacked by Sunset and survived, Jeff felt he was ready for just about anything. But not on the little Brewer.

During the summer of 1962 Dick Brewer made him a second board, a nine feet two inch gun, nineteen inches wide and two and seven eighths thick - "considered a dart in those times", Dick Brewer says today. Nobody had two surfboards in those days, let alone two Brewers at thirteen years of age! Even the hero big wave riders at Sunset and Waimea often rode the same favoured boards, year in, year out. By the end of the decade no surfer worth the salt in his ears would even contemplate a winter season in Hawaii without a full quiver of boards covering all conceivable conditions. But the winds of change had only just begun to blow through the Hawaiian surfing scene, and cool Dick Brewer and little Jeff Hakman were in their vanguard.

The outlaw lifestyle of the pioneer surfers, with their hard drinking, wild driving, crazy womanising and no-tomorrow attitude would continue to dominate the public perception of surfing (and, to an extent, the reality of life on the North Shore) but by 1962 a new style of surfer was emerging, and with it a new approach to wave riding.

The best examples of the new wave were probably Paul Strauch Jr, Joey Cabell, Phil Edwards and John Peck, all Californians, except Strauch, who was born and raised in Hawaii. What made these surfers different was that they were hot-doggers – small wave artists who had simply moved their acts to a bigger canvas. Strauch, an inspiration to Jeff, was a beautifully elegant surfer whose poise never changed regardless of the size of the wave. Cabell was as good a skier as he was a surfer, and he brought to surfing a parallel stance style in which weight distribution and subtle direction changes made perfect positioning look easy. Edwards was also a fluid mover who seemed indifferent to wave size. He was the first to surf big Pipeline in December 1961, but the following winter it was Peck who made the place his own, arching into flowing turns and grabbing the rail of his board to blast through tight sections – standard today, but revolutionary in 1962.

Jeff at Laniakea, 1961.

The birth of style, 1961.

Harry had started a new job as a machinery designer at Dole Pineapple, and had less time to surf, but when the first swells of the season came, he and Jeff were invariably on the road to the North Shore come dawn on Saturday. As they drove past Wahiawa one day in late October, prior to starting the pretty descent through the cane fields to Haleiwa, they noticed a flurry of activity at Schofield Barracks, armoured trucks pulling out and troops on the move. Later in the day they discovered that President Kennedy had ordered the US Navy to blockade Cuba and intercept Soviet ships carrying missiles. The entire American defence force was on full red alert and poised for nuclear war. On the positive side, the new Brewer went real well at overhead Laniakea.

The Australians arrived for the first time that winter, signifying the beginning of a new international era on the North Shore. Prior to going to Makaha for the contest, Bernard "Midget" Farrelly, Bob Pike, Dave Jackman and their moviemaker friend Bob Evans surfed up and down the strip. While Pike and Jackman were clearly big wave specialists in the old style, Farrelly had a whippy, Californian approach to hot-dogging, which he combined with an intensity of purpose that was almost frightening. He also had definite ideas about his equipment, stressing the importance of lightness, totally contradictory to the conventional North Shore wisdom that big waves required heavy boards.

Farrelly went on to win the Makaha meet in small to medium surf that year, but Jeff was not there to see it. Despite the fact that his Punahou colleague Freddy Hemmings had won the junior title the year before, and friends like Jackie Eberle were convinced that he would do well, Jeff had already decided that he was more interested in surfing the North Shore than in competing. Says Harry Hakman: "If everyone was at Makaha, Jeff sure knew where he wanted to be – Sunset."

Early in the new year Waimea Bay broke, twenty feet solid with bigger sets. Jeff and Harry watched it for a while, then Harry said: "I don't know about you, but I'm going out". He began taking his board off the car. Jeff had seen Waimea break two or three times before this and stayed on the cliff, but he had the Brewer gun now, he had no excuses.

"Yeah, me too."

To put this in perspective, a twenty foot wave is a monster of a thing. In the 1990s extreme surfers are being towed by jet ski into open ocean waves more than twice that size, but to this day no one has ever paddled, unaided, into a wave bigger than thirty feet and survived the elevator drop. Indeed, several surfers have been killed in the attempt to ride the biggest wave. In January 1963, when Jeff Hakman surfed Waimea Bay for the first time, at twenty feet plus, the place had only been surfed successfully for six winters, mostly by the same dozen or so crazed hellraisers in their twenties and thirties. When he timed his run through the shorebreak that morning and paddled out to the lineup, Jeff was just fourteen years and six weeks old, not yet five feet tall nor one hundred pounds in weight.

He recalls: "As I paddled out I had the theme from Peter Gunn in my head, couldn't get rid of it. It was the music for this horrible wipeout scene in one of the really old surf movies, guys just eating it. I was scared enough already and it didn't help."

Peter Cole, one of his teachers from Punahou, was in the lineup, along with Greg Noll, Buzzy Trent, Kealoha Kaio and the local school principal, Jose Angel, a charming man Harry had already become friendly with through their mutual interest in diving. Jeff took his time, getting the rhythm of the masses of moving water underneath him. He took his place in the pecking order, watching as the big men stroked powerfully down the faces of the monster waves, then disappeared from view as the entire bay seemed to errupt. Finally, he was in place for a smaller wave, perhaps eighteen feet. He swung the Brewer around and paddled as hard as he could.

Jeff stroked one more time as he felt the power of the wave lifting him, then stood cleanly with knees bent to absorb the drop. From the bottom of the wave he steered a safe passage to the channel and pulled out. Nothing to it. He paddled back out considerably

Looking for that big cutback, Haleiwa, 1961.

relieved. The big wave riders were talking to him now. "Hey, kid, made that one okay, huh?" The ice had been broken. Now he was part of the Waimea club too.

Jeff waited through several sets, until he judged a wave was rightfully his. When the next set approached, he paddled deeper inside and began to stroke for it. This one was at least four feet bigger than his first wave, and as he made the long, bumpy drop he realised that he had confused ambition with ability. He drove hard for the shoulder but the curtain came over and he was blasted from his board.

"After my experience at Sunset, I expected to be driven under for a long time, and to come up with nothing left in my lungs and another wave about to break on me. But it wasn't like that. I skimmed across the surface of the water like a stone. I was moving too fast to penetrate the water. I just kept getting tumbled over and over, then finally I went under, but it wasn't as bad as I'd feared. I bobbed up okay. Waimea is often like that. If you're driving along the face of the thing, by the time you get blasted it's already backing into the deeper water and you can survive it. It's when you're way back inside and blow it that you're in big trouble."

Jeff's confidence grew with every wave that day, and just as he contemplated going in, another set presented itself. Better late than never, he realised that no one was paddling for the first wave. He swung his board around and dug deep. He kept stroking even when he knew he'd missed the wave, because a gut instinct told him what to expect when he turned around. This was every surfer's nightmare, and the reason the first wave of a very big set was sometimes left unridden. Often the first wave was pushing a lot of water in front of it, making it harder to get into, and failure to do so meant being thirty or forty feet too far inside to paddle over the four or five huge waves behind it.

This was the dilemma Jeff faced as he stared at the twenty-five feet wall of water feathering in front of him, and paddled furiously towards it.

"I remember thinking, this is it, Jeff. You're dead. I couldn't see anybody else around, it was a very lonely feeling. The boards in those days, you couldn't duck dive or punch through

First surf at Waimea Bay, 1963.

the lip. The only thing you could do, and it only ever worked if there was enough offshore wind, was to stand up on your board as you got sucked up the face of the breaking wave, and try to kick it through the lip and into the air. I figured it was my only chance, so I stood up under the lip and kicked it like crazy in the direction of the channel. I fell back down the face, got churned violently for a moment, then spat out the back of the wave, and my board was there. I couldn't believe my luck. Another fifteen feet inside and I would have been nailed and gone real deep. I'm not sure that I could have held my breath for as long as it takes at that stage. From that day on I knew exactly where to sit at Waimea, and I wouldn't allow myself to get drawn too far inside for anyone."

Right at the end of that winter there was one last big swell. Harry knocked off work early and picked up Jeff from school and they raced to the North Shore to get a surf in before dark. Waimea was breaking fifteen to eighteen feet, but the swell was not quite strong enough to make it right, so they drove on to Sunset. Fred Van Dyke, who had driven just as fast from Punahou, was the only surfer in the car park. He looked at Jeff and Harry, shook his head and said: "Too big for me."

Van Dyke was in peak physical condition, a waterman who was there in the lineup on the biggest rideable days at both Sunset and Waimea, but his call on this windless and eery afternoon was that Sunset was too big to ride. Jeff and Harry peered out into the misty, smoking lineup. It was huge, perhaps twenty feet, with northwest bowls breaking way out on the second reef. But they were perfectly formed, and from the safety of the beach, Jeff could imagine himself driving, driving into the bottomless pit, then carving perhaps the biggest bottom turn in history to come smoking out of the barrel. If it was the fantasy of an over-amped schoolboy, then it was shared by the schoolboy's father.

Harry said, "Let's give it a try".

Father and son paddled out in the gloom, leaving behind an empty, lonely beach. They had perhaps an hour before total darkness.

Jeff: "It was much bigger than we'd thought, and we'd thought it was huge! It was unusually glassy and so much water was moving around, it was almost impossible to line it up. You'd see these things break out on the horizon and then come through and reform on the reef. We scratched around dodging sets for about fifty minutes without catching a wave. The sun was starting to set and I was determined to catch one before it got dark, so I took the risk and paddled further inside as a set approached. I wasn't quite into position for the first one, about fifteen feet, so I pulled back from paddling for it, swung around and stroked over the top. The next one was just huge, sucking and converging as it hit the reef. I really wanted to keep paddling over it to safety, but I knew this was my last chance to catch a wave. So I held my ground and started paddling. By the time it got to me it was so steep that I was totally committed, couldn't back out if I tried, and I was terrified.

"I'd caught bigger waves, but nothing even remotely as powerful as this. It had the dimensions of an A-frame house and it was moving real, real fast. As I paddled I thought, if I blow this I'll probably drown and no one will know. I only looked over my shoulder once, just to make sure it wasn't going to explode on my head, then it picked me up and sucked me into its vortex, and suddenly I'm flying down the face. I don't think there was much fin in the water. The board just seemed to fall straight down the face but it held its line and I stayed on my feet. As the wave converged it made this dreadful sucking noise and just drew me into it. All I could do was try to stay on and hold trim. It sucked me up into it about three times, totally in control of my destiny, then it just blew apart and spat me out into the channel.

"I'd never felt so exhilarated in my life! It was just such a fantastic feeling to have made that commitment and survived. Every second I rode that wave I was on the edge of falling off, barely in control. I'd pushed the limits of my ability, maybe of anyone's, and made it."

Jeff paddled into the beach and waited for his father, still paddling in from the lineup. It was completely dark as they walked back to the car. Jeff didn't say a word about the wave, but his body tingled all over and he'd never felt so alive.

Opposite: Dr Don James' classic portrait of Jeff at Sunset, 1963.

37

CHAPTER 7

Gnarly Sunset, 1962.

In the summer of 1963 the Hakmans built a modest A-frame in the front of the break known as Log Cabins and moved out to the North Shore. Doris, who'd become very involved with her Honolulu tennis circle and had both the girls taking lessons, was not particularly pleased with the idea, but Harry convinced her that it made a lot of sense. The cost of living was cheaper, the area was becoming quite civilised, and Jeff would soon be old enough to drive (fifteen) and then he could drop Harry off at Dole Pineapple and continue on to Punahou. Besides, there were tennis courts at Haleiwa, everything would be fine.

Once they'd established their new home, Harry developed friendships with many of the local big wave riders and watermen. Jose Angel was a special friend, and he also got quite close to Ricky Grigg, who'd turned his love of the ocean into a scientific career at the Scripps Institute.

The previous winter Grigg had accompanied Harry's photographer friend, Ron Church, on a surfing and photographic safari to Maui. Grigg now had some of the results hanging in his living room – beautiful colour prints of Honolua Bay shot from the water.

One day on a visit, Jeff's jaw dropped as he looked at the immaculate waves breaking in one of the most beautiful bays in the world. "Where is this place?" he asked. He made a mental note of the name.

Ironically, a few weeks later he was contacted by a movie-maker named Dale Davis, or "Frail Dale" as the diminutive photographer was known to the surfers. Davis was putting a surfing trip together to shoot footage for his new movie. Brewer, Freddy Hemmings and Kiki Spangler were on the team, was Jeff in?

"Depends, where we goin'?"

"Honolua Bay."

"I'm there!"

The team met at the airport for the short hop to Maui. Brewer had brought his wife, Betty, along for the trip. Jeff didn't know too much about Betty, but he was in awe of her.

The North Shore surfers called her Sweaty Betty, for no reason other than that it rhymed, and it was said that Brewer, the coolest of cool, the guru shaper, was scared shitless of her.

One day Jeff had been in Brewer's filthy shaping bay at Haleiwa with some other guys, all knee-deep in foam shavings, when Betty's rasping voice rang out through the shop. "Dick, where are you? I want to speak with you, Dick. Dick! Diiiick!"

She was getting closer. Jeff looked on in amazement as Brewer dived into the foam and covered himself with it. Betty appeared at the door of the bay. Jeff and the others shook their heads. Not here. The voice trailed off as she continued the search elsewhere. Brewer got up, dusted himself down and resumed shaping.

Honolua failed to live up to expectations, but Frail Dale got some okay footage of the boys surfing the inside bowl and was happy enough. Betty was in a playful mood as they waited in the small airport terminal for the flight back to Oahu. She had a baby's blanket wrapped up into a tight parcel on her lap. "Look at my little baby, Dick", she purred. "Diiick! Look at my little baby, goddammit!"

Dick said: "Nice little baby, cootchy, cootchy, coo".

She kept it up when the plane arrived and clutched the baby to her chest as she boarded. Jeff heard the stewardess compliment her on having such a quiet and well-behaved

Dick and Betty Brewer, Honolua Bay, 1967.

JOHN WITZIG

baby, and thought that the joke was getting a little weird. When the plane arrived at Honolulu, two stewards helped the passengers down the rear stairs and onto the tarmac. Betty and her "baby" were the last to deplane. As she stood at the top of the stairs, Brewer turned around in the high trade wind and called, "Honey, throw me the baby!"

Betty let out a mad cackle and hurled the blanket towards the tarmac. In that split second the two stewards dived towards the small package, one of them smashing his hip against the guard-rail and crashing hard on the tarmac. The blanket fell to earth, where Betty picked it up and strode towards the terminal without looking back. She was still laughing about it weeks later.

As well as being shaper to the brave and dangerous, and cultural guru to the North Shore, Dick Brewer became the instigator and organiser of regular surfing contests at Haleiwa. These were low-profile events, but they often attracted a galaxy of stars in the making. Jeff found himself surfing against the likes of Jackie Eberle, Kiki Spangler, Jimmy Lucas, Ryan Dotson, Jay Clarke and John Peck. Barry Kanaiaupuni, who had been the outstanding surfer at Queens the previous summer, was living in California and temporarily out of the picture. Jeff enjoyed surfing with the best of the new breed in Hawaii, but he had not yet developed a competitive nature. He preferred the very private challenge of surfing beyond the limitations of his size, skill and experience. He liked the edge, and in that he had an affinity with the pioneer big wave riders on the North Shore.

In fact he had become very close to several of the leading lights, especially his father's friend Jose Angel and his teachers at Punahou, Ricky Grigg, Fred Van Dyke and Peter Cole. Grigg, Van Dyke and Cole had all surfed Steamer Lane and Pleasure Point in Santa Cruz together back in the early 1950s, and when Van Dyke relocated to Hawaii, his buddies soon followed. The three teachers shared a house on the North Shore from 1958 to '61, seminal years in big wave riding when each played an important role.

Tall, softly spoken Peter Cole was Jeff's algebra teacher and his favourite. "Mr Cole" would often turn up for class with his hair still wet and salt caked all over his face after a session at Ala Moana. He had even been known to cite in Chapel a fifteen feet Sunset west swell as evidence of God's bountiful grace. Cole was a kind of loveable, nutty professor type. Sitting in his living room at Rocky Point in 1996, he told this writer: "Jeff was always smiling in class, or maybe he was laughing at me. I was a screw-up of a teacher. I'd always get more chalk on me than on the board."

Between 1960 and '65 Cole's student roll read like a who's who of the surfing world: Paul Strauch Jr, Fred Hemmings, Gerry Lopez, Jimmy Blears, James Jones, Jeff Hakman...and not many of them were straight A students. Says Cole: "It was hard to get them motivated if they were addicted to surfing. Hemmings was the worst math student I ever had. He was working nights parking cars in Waikiki, and he'd come into class totally zonked. One day he fell asleep right in the middle of my lesson. I just kept on talking real quiet so as not to disturb him. When the lesson was over I got my students to leave real quiet too, and Fred just kept on snoring. Halfway through the third class I couldn't stand it any longer. I yelled at him and woke him up.

"Lopez, on the other hand, was a very good math student but we didn't know he was a good surfer. He was just this real quiet, shy guy who worked very hard. When Gerry went on to become a great surfer it came as a bit of a shock.

"Jeff didn't pick up on math too well. I think I gave him a C plus, and that was being generous. But he was very bright, and a really nice kid."

Fred Van Dyke taught Jeff science. He too was a courageous big wave rider, but his persona on land was a little unusual. Van Dyke was fanatical about diet, health and the environment long before they became fashionable issues. At Punahou he spent his entire lunch hour swimming against a bungy cord in the school pool. He ate wheatgerm oil and brewer's yeast with soy beans. He was passionate about things no one cared about, and he wore a gas mask when he drove his Volkswagen bug. Always his own man, Van Dyke endeared him-

RCN CHURCH

Above: Cheater five, or "Strauch stretch".
Left: Surfing buddies, Jeff and Harry.

self to the North Shore surfing fraternity when he told *Sports Illustrated* magazine that most big wave riders were latent homosexuals.

Cole, Van Dyke, the Hakmans and several other North Shore commuters were part of a car pool in those pre-freeway days when it could take as long as three hours to drive from Sunset Beach to Honolulu. Peter Cole remembers: "It could be a really bad drive, particularly if the weather was bad or there was an accident. The traffic would just pile up about five or six miles the country side of Pearl City, and we'd be sitting there bumper to bumper, Fred wearing his gas mask. Sometimes there'd be three or four carloads of us, and we knew this short cut through the sugar cane fields. It was just this little dirt track and we'd be hurtling along it in convoy. There was a chain across the track about halfway along, and the passenger in the first car would jump out and hold it up while all the cars went through, then jump back in the last car. You can imagine all this happening at a million miles an hour coming home on those winter afternoons when there was big surf."

But Peter Cole rarely beat the traffic home in time to get a late surf. Increasingly frustrated at missing out on the best swells, he kept Fred Hemmings awake long enough to graduate in 1965, then left Punahou for a job in the civil service.

In the early part of 1964, Jeff became friendly with a surfer named Barry Bloomfield, and his brother Harold, a wild kind of guy a few years older. Barry was frequently in the lineup at Ala Moana, while Harold seemed very popular with many of the surfers hanging around in the car park. Jeff noticed that he sometimes rolled his own cigarettes and then shared them with the other guys. Harold Bloomfield's other passion was screwing up military manoeuvres in the hills behind Pupukea. The army had stepped up its training exercises in response to a widening conflict in some place called Vietnam, and Harold's idea of fun was to share a few cigarettes with the guys, then get on his motor bike and go terrorise a group of rookie soldiers. He had a collection of military weaponry and a big scar on his back where he claimed to have been shot.

The talk around Ala Mo was of a Malibu-style lefthand wave on Kauai that hardly anyone knew about. It was called Infinities. Surfers Roy Mesker and Chris Green put together a little crew to go surf it and invited Jeff to join them. Before they even had their first surf at Infinities however, they ran into Harold Bloomfield, who rolled a huge cigarette, took a few puffs and passed it to Jeff, who declined. "No thanks, I don't smoke."

"Jeff, do you know what this is?"

"Nope."

"It's pot, Jeff. Marijuana. It'll blow your fuckin' mind, man. It'll change your life. You'll surf better than you ever have and you'll never be the same again."

Jeff gingerly took a drag and passed it on. He recalls: "I'd just started to have a beer now and then. I was totally raw and this was my first exposure to drugs of any kind. I remember feeling kind of fuzzy and dopey for a while. I suppose I was loaded but it didn't impress me very much. The other guys stayed pretty much loaded for a week."

The marijuana Jeff tried was probably a Thai variety, brought back from Vietnam by one of the thousands of servicemen who passed through Oahu. But, as Bob Dylan had sung, the times, they were a changing, and within the year marijuana would be a huge cash crop grown throughout the Hawaiian islands, and a whole generation would be tuning in and turning on to an entire range of psychotropic substances. And surfing's hellmen, always on the lookout for a new buzz, would be in the front line.

CHAPTER 8

LeROY GRANNIS

By 1964 Dick Brewer and his Surfboards Hawaii decal had become famous throughout the surfing world. His name was synonymous with quality construction and high peformance in big waves. In other words, the purchase of a Brewer was a ticket to the big time.

Of course, not every surfer had the technique to extract the best performance from Brewer's shapes, which even then were a great deal more subtle than the majority of logs being punched out to satisfy the huge and growing market as surfing reached its commercial zenith. But that didn't matter. If you had a Brewer you were on your way. The only problem was that it was almost impossible to get one if you were not a top name surfer.

Then, during the winter season of 1963-4, it became impossible to get a custom-made Brewer or any other surfboard in Hawaii, owing to a Matson Shipping Line strike which halted the importation of blanks from the mainland. In California a surfer and businessman named John Price had negotiated a deal with Brewer to manufacture boards under the Surfboards Hawaii label in Encinitas, near San Diego. So, as the summer vacation approached and the strike dragged on, Dick Brewer decided to close his Haleiwa shop and head for the mainland. He asked Jeff if he'd like to go to California to do some promotions as a Surfboards Hawaii team rider, and also work for John Price in his retail store. Jeff jumped at the chance.

Hawaii may have been the spiritual home of surfing, but by 1964 the Surf City that Jan and Dean sang about was Southern California. The lightness of being that Jeff had sensed in 1959 was now a full-blown surf craze. From the South Bay to the Tijuana Sloughs, surfers were god, man. They had the moves, the boards, the cars and, of course, they had the chicks. And the surfers who had the most of everything were the team riders, the heroes whose photos appeared in the surfing magazines and who could be seen carving at exotic locations in the surf movies, which were now being pumped out at the rate of one a month. Even Hollywood was churning out surf epics, like the ludicrous Ride The Wild Surf.

In May 1964 Australia's Midget Farrelly had pipped Joey Cabell to become the first

Jeff and his Brewer Surfboards Hawaii semi-gun, 1965.

official world champion surfer at Manly Beach in Sydney, but back in California this may as well have taken place in a different galaxy. Everyone knew that either Phil Edwards or Dewey Weber was the best surfer in the world, with Mickey Dora, Corky Carroll, Rusty Miller and a host of others just behind.

When Jeff arrived back in California he was astounded at how commercialised surfing had become. When he had left to go to Hawaii, surfers were still very much outlaws, rebels on the fringe of society. Now everyone under twenty-five, male or female, was a surfer, or at least looked like one. Surf shops had sprung up on every corner in the beachside sub-urbs – even in inland Orange County and the San Fernando Valley – and the radio stations played surf music nonstop. The whole scene was out of control, and Jeff loved it.

John Price put him up at his own house right above the beach at Leucadia. Says Jeff: "All I had to do was roll out of bed and down the cliff and into the surf. I had to do a little bit of work here and there, but mostly it was just surf, parties and chicks. I had a crush on Irene the surf queen. She was blonde and tanned and she surfed a bit. I was just in awe. We didn't have beach bunnies like that in Hawaii."

Jeff had his licence and access to a car, so he could cruise the coast looking for surf, and even slip down to Mexico and surf the uncrowded spots in Baja. And when Brewer shaped him a new board which was ideal for Californian conditions, he was in hog's heaven. To keep up his profile as a team rider, Jeff entered several contests and surprised himself by winning at Windansea, Solana Beach and San Miguel in Mexico.

One of Jeff's less pleasing jobs that summer was to babysit toddler Laird Hamilton, later to become the totally fearless king of "tow-in" surfing. Little Laird was an uncompromising individual even then. One night as Jeff dozed on the other side of the room, Laird hurled a Coke bottle from his crib and cracked the window. Jeff woke up with a start. No, surely a baby couldn't do that? But he had.

The glasser at Surfboards Hawaii had a GTO which was the fastest means of getting to Baja. Every couple of days he and Jeff would throw their boards in the back, turn Bob Dylan up on the tape deck and roar south down the freeway, passing a joint as they drove. Dope had not yet permeated the mainstream surf culture, but around the hip surf shops there was plenty, and despite his reservations, Jeff smoked it fairly frequently. "I'd smoke it to be sociable, but it just wasn't my poison really. And I still had this thing about the drug addicts of San Pedro. I'd grown up with my father pointing out these bums to me, the guys who had started out smoking marijuana and had ended up on heroin. That was my condition-ing, so I was very wary of the stuff."

In his sophomore year at Punahou, 1964-65, Jeff firmly established himself as Hawaii's hottest young surfer. Surfing big Sunset remained his real passion, but the summer in California had turned him into a complete performer, and on the North Shore he was pretty much in a class of his own. Pretty much because a gawky kid called Jock Sutherland had also suddenly emerged as a quality surfer in all sized waves. A goofy footer, young Jock was a superb switch-footer who could actually carve a bottom turn on a big wave in switched stance. At the time many of the better goofy foot surfers switched feet to tuck into the face of the wave, but few were good enough to be called totally ambidexterous. Jock was.

His style was perhaps less pleasing on the eye than Jeff's, but Jock seldom caught a wave without doing something totally amazing. He could even move vertically which, considering the limitations of the equipment of the day, was beyond amazing. He and Jeff soon became close friends.

The limitations of equipment were starting to bug Jeff. By 1965 Brewer had sold Surfboards Hawaii and moved into a shop in Wahiawa under the Hobie label. Jeff was still on the Brewer team, along with Jackie Eberle, Kiki Spangler and Jimmy Lucas, but Brewer had gone off on a tangent with his coloured foam concaves. They were the most expen-sive boards in the world, and were considered by many surfers to be the Ferraris of the surf. But they didn't work for Jeff.

"They were sure fast, but you had to turn them on the flat or not at all, and I had real problems making them go. So I experimented with all kinds of designs during the summer, but it wasn't until fall that year that Brewer made me a ten feet one inch gun with a flat bottom, no concave, that I felt comfortable and confident again."

That summer Jeff's friend Chris Green and some of the other stone freak surfers had started raving about a new drug experience, something that elevated surfing, even more than pot did, into a quasi-religious experience. The drug was called LSD, or more properly lysergic acid diethylamide, or even just acid, and its high priest was a former academic named Timothy Leary. In the summer of '65 Leary and cohorts like the writer Ken Kesey were trumpeting the mind-expanding properties of this new hallucinogenic in San Francisco, then the capital of the Beat Generation. In Hawaii, capital of the Surf Generation, people like Chris Green and Harold Bloomfield were quick to pick up on the idea and find a supply.

Bloomfield was a left-field kind of guy, the type you'd expect to experiment, but Jeff also began to see that some of the leading surfers were acid-heads. People whose ability he respected beyond most others were suddenly full of acid raves. Jeff's good friend Jackie Eberle and John Peck, for example, could speak of little else. But by far the biggest devotee was Paul Gebauer, a naturally talented and stylish surfer who Jeff ranked up near Paul Strauch when it came to North Shore performances in the early 1960s, particularly at Sunset Beach.

Gebauer was probably the first North Shore acid guru. The drug became his religion and he moved to Maui and spent much of his time in the Haleakala Crater communing with extraterrestrials.

Through Harold Bloomfield and other friends like Chris Green and Kiki Spangler, Jeff was induced to try LSD. They dropped purple Owsley tabs and walked up into the mountains and watched the sun set over the sea. After his marijuana experiences, Jeff's expectations were low, but he liked the surge of adrenalin he felt on LSD, and the tricks it played with his mind. "It seemed to change the way you visualised things, and I remember liking it very much, except that I felt totally drained when the trip was over. But it was a drug that did something for me, and whereas I could take or leave pot, LSD intrigued me."

Jeff, Jock Sutherland and Jackie Eberle began surfing on LSD. They would score on a Friday, drop the tab on Saturday morning and go out surfing, regardless of whether it was four feet or twenty feet. Says Jeff: "I didn't do it too many times, but I found it actually enhanced the energy level out there. It was quite tranquil and very entertaining, what with the colours and all. I mean I would never take so much I was a giggling mess, but I liked the slight distortion, you know, that was fun.

"Some of my friends would really take a lot, to the point where they had no idea what they were doing in the surf. They'd be cruising along on the shoulder in another dimension and they'd paddle back out and tell you how far out the wave was. They just didn't know. I was pretty conservative with it, I kept it in check. A couple of times I remember surfing big Sunset and Waimea when I was tripping, but that was later."

What dimension was John Peck in when he wrote of a Waimea experience: "I knifed through velvet darkness on wings of sleep. My subconscious: soft, secretive palms caressed by warm and gentle trades merged and mingled with plumes of skyward hissing spray...the afterbirth of huge resplendent north swells overflowing into drives of aggressiveness and yearning, a craving...for its voice."

By 1968 surfing magazines would be filled with acid rave nonsense, but in 1965 Jeff's buddies were at the leading edge of dope consciousness, poised to go higher and higher before the inevitable plunge to earth.

CHAPTER 9

Classic positioning at Sunset, 1965.

Driving to school in the car pool one day in the fall of 1965, Fred Van Dyke mentioned to Jeff that he had been approached by Honolulu businessman and nightclub entrepreneur Kimo Wilder McVay to put together a professional surfing contest to be held on the North Shore that coming winter.

McVay's idea was to gather the best surfers in the world at the premier surf location in the world, unleash them when conditions were right and let a television crew film it for a worldwide audience. The contest, to be called the Duke Kahanamoku Invitational, would pay tribute to the modern day godfather of Hawaiian surfing, Duke Paoa Kahanamoku, while perhaps also drawing a little attention to Duke Kahanamoku's, the nightclub McVay had set up in the great man's name at the International Market Place in Waikiki.

Jeff was intrigued, but he had no idea what Van Dyke was talking about. "A professional surfing contest? Like you get paid money to go surfing?"

"That's right, Jeff. Interested?"

"You mean like I'd be invited?"

"If you want I'll put your name up and I'm sure it will be accepted."

"Shoot, really?"

"Yeah, really."

Jeff recalls: "I couldn't believe I was really going to be invited. It just didn't seem possible. I thought it would be just such an incredible honour, and I really hadn't done much in contest surfing. I'd been in the Makaha contest one year and I'd won a couple of minor meets in California and Mexico, and that was it. So, you know, Fred tended to go on a bit at times, so I just put the whole thing out of my mind."

On November 6, 1965, the secretary of the dean of Punahou School handed Jeff an official-looking envelope. As he walked to class Jeff tore open the letter. Shit, he wasn't being expelled, just because he'd experimented with drugs! It didn't seem fair. Everyone was doing it!

But the official looking letter was not from Punahou. The letterhead featured a shield with a surfer performing an elegant cutback on the right side. It was from the Duke Kahanomoku Invitational Surfing Championships, and it was headed, "Jeff Hackman, Esq."

"Congratulations on your being selected as one of the world's top 24 surfers to compete in the first annual Duke Kahanamoku Invitational Surfing Championships, December 14 to 17, 1965. Although this is a 'first annual', CBS-TV has contracted to film the event in color to broadcast nationally...Bruce Brown has been retained by CBS to help with the filming...You will be the guest of Sheraton's beautiful Surfrider Hotel at Waikiki Beach...your transportation to the Islands will be provided and you will receive $50 to help defray the cost of meals and other expenses..."

The letter went on to outline a heavy agenda of social events, starting with a press conference and dinner at Duke Kahanamoku's (including the Don Ho Show) and concluding with an absolute extravaganza awards ceremony at the Waikiki Shell. Jeff stared at the letter in amazement. Surfing had never, ever had anything like this. Acceptance, respectability...Jesus, fifty bucks spending money!

Kimo Wilder McVay was, in the nicest possible way, a hustler. Jeff, who'd never met him prior to the contest, later described him as a "whisky and cigarettes kind of guy". In other words Kimo wasn't very surf, and yet he'd taken on as his responsibility the financial welfare of Duke Kahanamoku who, despite his triumphant sporting career in swimming pool and surf, had not used his money wisely. In 1965, Duke's seventy-fifth year, the nightclub that bore his name was the hottest place in town, with tourists flocking to the Don Ho Show every night, and McVay made sure Duke got looked after with the proceeds.

For the world's first professional surfing contest (no prize money but an appearance fee) Kimo McVay secured the sponsorship of not only the luxurious beachfront Sheraton Surfrider Hotel at Waikiki, but of San Francisco's Lucky Lager, "the beer beer drinkers drink". When the 24 invited surfers began checking into the Surfrider on Monday, December 13, to find a case of Lucky in each room, they immediately began to prove that it was also the beer that surfers drink.

The invitees were an interesting mix of respected pioneer big wave riders, California's finest and a sprinkling of young hotties from Hawaii and the mainland. But there was only one non-American – Peruvian Felipe Pomar, the 1965 world amateur champion and a Hawaiian college student. The 1964 world champion, Australia's Midget Farrelly had been overlooked despite impressive performances in Hawaiian waves, including a victory in the 1962 Makaha meet. The other notable omission from Australia was Nat Young, who had finished second to Pomar in the world titles in a controversial final at Punta Rocas, Peru, and was widely regarded as one of the best young surfers in the world.

Nevertheless, Fred Van Dyke and his judging panel believed they had a representative sample of the world's best, with big wave experts like Peter Cole, Greg Noll and George Downing, small wave performers like Mickey Dora, Skip Frye and Dewey Weber, and the new breed inclusions like Corky Carroll, Fred Hemmings, Jackie Eberle and Jeff Hakman. The judging panel of Wally Froiseth, Mark Martinson and Buzzy Trent was also meant to reflect this mix, with one judge representing the new, the old and the big wave crazies.

Jeff checked into the Surfrider as instructed and found that he was sharing a room with Mickey Munoz, the head-dipping hotdogger from California who, at five feet four, was the only person in the contest who was shorter than Jeff. Munoz was sprawled on his bed, sipping a Lucky. "You wanna beer?" he greeted Jeff. "How cool is this?" It was pretty cool. Jeff opened a beer and checked out his book of restaurant coupons and his free clothes.

By the end of the afternoon a full party was in progress, with Greg Noll leading the Californians on to more and more outrages. Says Jeff: "I don't remember anything real bad happening, it was just the usual pranks. But there were two groups of surfers. One was the older guys who were into boozing and having a good time, and the other was the young guys who were more into pot and psychedelics. John Peck couldn't stop talking about his

All this and fifty bucks spending money!

acid trips, and it drove Fred Hemmings nuts. He just couldn't believe that surfers would take drugs and it appalled him."

The format of the Duke Invitational was simple enough – four heats of six to hit the water whenever the waves were good on the North Shore within the four-day waiting period, the top two surfers in each heat to advance to an eight-man final. Van Dyke estimated that the entire contest could be conducted in one day, giving all the surfers equal opportunity in the prevailing conditions.

When the surfers, sponsors and organisers met for yet another boozy celebration at Duke's nightclub on the Tuesday night, the word was that the swell was on the way. This was a considerable relief for Jeff, who was ill at ease with the media attention and the hoopla, and just wanted to get on with it. But the party rowdies were undeterred and some of the surfers who showed up for the bus ride to the North Shore at six the next morning looked a little worse for wear. Jeff was not one of them. He felt fit and amped up to surf well.

Says Peter Cole: "Anyone who'd seen Jeff surf Sunset Beach knew he was a very serious contender for this contest. Some of the big name Californians might not have known, and the press certainly didn't know, but we knew he was the guy to beat."

Sunset was eight to ten feet and ugly, with shifting peaks and an erratic west swell making it difficult to surf. Peter Cole and some other regulars urged Van Dyke to hold off, but with the CBS crew agape at the biggest and best waves they had ever seen, and the difficult conditions ensuring plenty of spectacular wipeouts, the first Duke meet was on.

Jeff hit the water in the first heat on his ten feet one inch Brewer gun, a beautifully-constructed board with a narrow tail and four redwood stringers. He was up against Kimo Hollinger, Mike Hynson, Joey Cabell, Mickey Dora and Rusty Miller. Of these Hollinger had probably clocked the most water time at Sunset, but Rusty Miller had been exceptional there the previous winter, and Cabell was always capable of producing an utterly mind-blowing session. But Jeff blitzed them all, emerging a clear winner over Hollinger, with both advancing to the final.

As the day progressed the surf got cleaner with a strong trade wind, if a little smaller.

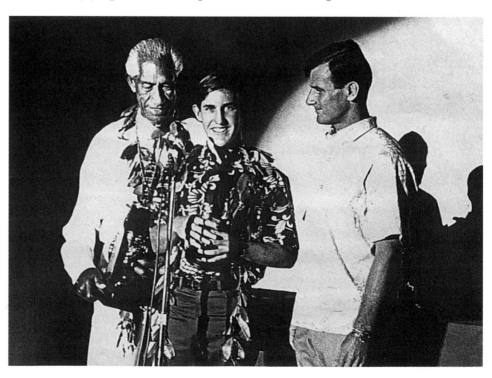

The first Duke champion with Duke Kahanamoku (left) and Fred Van Dyke.

RON STONER SEQUENCE

Two frames from Ron Stoner's classic sequence of Jeff's cheater five which won him the Duke title. "The best ride I ever saw at Sunset Beach", said Buzzy Trent.

Just after three, Jeff lined up for the beach start of the final with Kimo Hollinger, Paul Strauch, Felipe Pomar, Mike Doyle, Jackie Eberle, Bobby Cloutier and Corky Carroll. The break had shifted to Sunset Point, but every so often a bigger set would come through wide and break through to the bowl.

Jeff knee-paddled quickly to the point, beating the others into the lineup where he immediately picked up a small wave that peeled enough for him to get a tube ride. It was just the kind of positive start he needed. As he turned to paddle back out, a set came through wide and went unridden. Jeff changed his direction, swung left and paddled for the channel. Outside in the lineup, he sat alone and waited. The final was an hour long and would be judged on the best five waves. He only had one which would have been scored highly on performance but down on size. If he sat wide and nothing came through, he would be in trouble.

But the sets came. The first one was a solid eight feet. Jeff recalls: "I knew it was a good wave and that I really had to make it count. In those days you couldn't wind the board around. You could turn off the bottom but you couldn't really snap them all over the face.

The highest performance stuff you could do was to pick the line, ride as tight to the curl as possible and nose ride. So as I took off I played through what I could do to make the judges sit up and take notice. The big move of the day was the cheater five. You couldn't hang ten on a gun, but you could get up there and do a cheater and drive the thing from the nose. So I did that, and the wave just kept getting more and more critical. I dropped lower on the face and slowed down, and then speeded up again, and eventually made it right through the inside section, still on the nose. In a modern judging system I would have scored a ten for that wave. It was the best I could do, I was surfing above myself and when I heard people hooting on the beach I knew the judges would know that."

The sequence of Ron Stoner photographs which subsequently appeared in *Surfer* magazine shows Jeff perched on the nose, defying all odds and making section after section as the wave threatens to explode on his head. His confidence at an all-time high, he paddled back out and got another similar wave, although this time his cheater was abbreviated by a side chop that forced him back to the tail. By the time the other surfers realised that the Hakman kid was ripping out wide, it was too late. Not even Strauch, the man who had invented the cheater five and was Jeff's hero, could catch him.

When the points were tallied, Fred Van Dyke announced the placegetters from third up, and called them to a little makeshift podium in Val Valentine's backyard overlooking Sunset. Third was Felipe Pomar, second Paul Strauch. Jeff went bright red as Van Dyke stated the obvious. As Jeff moved forward to the podium, seventy-four-year-old Duke Kahanamoku clutched him in an emotional bear hug. Says Jeff: "I was overwhelmed. I mean I hardly knew Duke at that stage, but he seemed genuinely pleased that I had won his contest".

The judges had been unanimous, despite early differences of opinion, in awarding it to Jeff, a clear twenty-eight points ahead of Strauch. Froiseth commented: "Jeff surfed as good as anyone I've ever seen at Sunset Beach". Buzzy Trent said: "In my fifteen years at Sunset I've never seen anyone ride the waves better than Jeff. You just can't do better than that." Only Peter Cole disagreed. "Hell," he grinned, "Jeff wasn't even warmed up!"

On Friday night a fleet of limousines drove the surfers to the Waikiki Shell, where they received a standing ovation from the sellout crowd as they went on stage to accept their Duke statuettes. The surfers wore matching aloha shirts, and as they arrived models in grass skirts presented them with floral leis. During the formalities Mike Hynson, standing next to Jeff, made a whispered joke about wearing grass around your neck instead of smoking it.

When Jeff was called forward to receive his trophy, Fred Van Dyke whispered, "Say something, Jeff. Anything!"

"Ah, thanks everybody. I'm ah, stoked! Is that okay, Fred?"

Bruce Brown's new surf movie, Slippery When Wet was shown and then stomp band the Undertakers took to the stage and the dancing began. When Jeff and his girlfriend Linda Bickle walked into Duke Kahanamoku's nightclub around midnight a buzz went around the room. Wasn't that the little guy who beat all the top surfers?

It hadn't quite dawned on him yet, but Jeff Hakman had arrived in surfing's major league, and his life would never be the same again.

Small day at the Pipe, 1965.

CHAPTER 10

★ ★ ★ Thursday, Dec. 16, 1965 HONOLULU ADVERTISER B-5

Hakman Wins Surfing Title

By HAL WOOD
Advertiser Sports Editor

Jeff Hakman, a diminutive Hawaiian dare-devil, caught a "once in a lifetime" ride yesterday and hot-dogged his way with it to the Duke Kahanamoku Invitational Surfing championships at beautiful Sunset Beach.

Hakman, a baby-faced 17-year-old who stands only 5-4 and weighs 125 pounds with his surfing trunks dripping wet, beat 23 of the

up 219 points to win the event by a wide margin.

Paul Strauch Jr., also of Hawaii, finished second with 191 points, followed by Felipe Pomar of Peru with 184.

After a wash-out on Tuesday, meet director Fred Van Dyke flashed the "go" signal yesterday morning as waves of six to 10 feet rolled in at Sunset Beach and the caravan led by a CBS TV crew, headed for the show.

When the waves kept up,

The final standings:

Surfer Home	Points
1—Jeff Hakman, Hawaii	219
2—Paul Strauch Jr, Hawaii	191
3—Felipe Pomar, Peru	184
4—Jack Eberle, Hawaii	183
5—(Tie) Bob Cloutier, Hawaii	179
Mike Doyle, California	179
7—Corky Carroll, California	175
8—Kimo Hollinger, Hawaii	173

such as defending Makaha champion Fred Hemmings, who lost his board.

Many performed exceptionally well, but were nosed out in the judging by a point or two. Corky Car-

ger, Jack Eberle, and Bob Cloutier, all of Hawaii, and Mike Doyle and Carroll of California.

When the finals got under way at 3 p.m., the waves were hitting the 10 foot mark and it was here that Hakman, who is an all-around surfer, made his mark.

"It was a fantastic exhibition by Jeff," said Buzzy Trent, one of the judges. "That one ride he made was a one-in-a-million shot. He harnessed the wave. It was

junior division of a surfing tournament at Haleiwa last year. He was born in California, but has lived here for the past three years.

The young star wasn't overly excited by his triumph.

"I've surfed on better days," he said after the victory. "But that was the best ride I ever had."

Van Dyke said that after the horrible weather on Tuesday, the meet was fortunate to get the show completed

Local hero.

Jeff's Duke win catapulted him to international fame. He was featured in Time Magazine and when the CBS television special was aired in the spring, he was the star.

In the usual manner of these things, reporters hot for the local angle were quick to claim him. In Honolulu he was "Pun (Punahou) surfer surprise winner" and "diminutive Hawaiian dare-devil", in the Los Angeles Times he was "ex-Inglewood surfer" while in the New York Times he was "US unknown". It didn't matter to Jeff's maternal grandmother, Wilma ("Mrs G" to Jeff's surfing buddies). Back in Inglewood she started the first pages of a scrapbook of press cuttings. She optimistically labelled it "Volume One".

When he started back at Punahou after the Christmas break, he was called to Dean Metcalf's office and warmly congratulated. "If you need to miss some school to surf in contests," said the dean, "you come and see me". Jeff couldn't believe he was hearing this.

A couple of months after the contest, Kimo McVay phoned Jeff at the apartment his parents had rented back in town, and asked him to drop down to Duke Kahanamoku's for a beer and a chat. Jeff was shown into Kimo's office at the rear of the club and handed a Lucky Lager. Kimo had a whisky in one hand and a smoke in the other.

"Jeff, good of you to come down. You know Duke thinks a lot of you, right?"

Jeff nodded, a little embarrassed.

"Yeah, well he does, he thinks you're kinda special. Would you like to be on the Duke Kahanamoku Surf Team? Totally professional, boards, clothes, spending money, an account here at the club, you name it."

"But what do I have to do, Kimo?"

"Nothin' much. Just keep surfing the way you did in the meet, wear Duke's clothes, ride Duke's boards, maybe bring your girl down to the club some nights and meet some folks, just generally be Jeff Hakman, surf star."

It sounded like a deal to Jeff. He had been a Brewer team rider for a couple of years, of course, but this was very different. This was full page magazine ads, personal appearances with the other team members, this was like superstardom! The era of the team riders and the surf star models had well and truly arrived on the mainland, where Corky Carroll had his own model, David Nuuhiwa had his noserider, Dewey Weber had his "Performer", Greg Noll was putting the finishing touches to a Mickey Dora signature model called "Da Cat", Mike Doyle had a model with Hansen, Phil Edwards with Hobie, and even lesser lights like Dru Harrison and East Coaster Claude Codgen had their own models. But things had been a little slower to move in Hawaii, and the Duke team was the first real attempt to attract mainstream attention to a surf label.

In addition to Jeff, McVay had signed up Paul Strauch, Fred Hemmings, Joey Cabell and Butch Van Artsdalen. Later he added Jock Sutherland and Florida's Bruce Valluzzi. It was a strong team and it gave credibility to the whole marketing plan. Says Jeff: "We copped a lot of flak when we started wearing these aloha print shirts and jackets in team designs, but if you'd asked any surfer in Hawaii at that time if he'd like to be on the Duke Kahanamoku Surf Team, the answer would have been, you bet. It was a real honour."

McVay took out advertisements in the surfing magazines, selling five dollar memberships in the Duke Kahanamoku Surf Club. It didn't matter where you lived because there was no club as such, but the ads guaranteed you a membership card, a decal and an autographed team photo. They were rushed.

The only downer was the surfboards. McVay knew nothing about surfboards, but he knew a lot about business. You mass produced, you kept your unit price down, you got your products seen, you made a lot of money. But the massive, round-railed Duke Kahanamoku pop-outs were so heavy they couldn't be carried, and so poorly designed they couldn't be surfed. Says Jeff: "The boards were a total embarrassment. I had to tell Kimo I just couldn't do it, I had to have a Brewer under me."

Realising he had to try to salvage the situation, McVay hurriedly cut a deal with respected surfer and shaper Greg Noll, and by the end of 1966 the "new power combination" of the Duke Kahanamoku Surf Team and Greg Noll Surfboards had created the all new "Hawaiian Nollrider". None of the team riders had anything to do with the deal or

Above: The original Duke Kahanamoku Surf Team in an early ad.

Left: By 1966 the team included several of the hottest young surfers in the world, like Jeff and Jock Sutherland, either side of Duke. That's Kimo McVay with the smoke and the whisky.

Above: Top three at the Duke meet, Paul Strauch, Felipe Pomar and Jeff. (The following year they knew how to spell his name!)

Right: Jeff and Eddie Aikau paddling into the zone at Waimea Bay.

RON STONER

Above: International Surfing *magazine votes Jeff best big wave rider in the world, 1966.*

Below: Windansea Surf Club's Hawaiian contingent. Jeff centre, Jock second from right.

DICK FELDMAN

the subsequent surfboards, but the ads insisted: "Designer Paul Strauch has contributed in the nose riding department, while designer Jeff Hakman, through his good judgment, places special attention to trimming and edge control, whereas designer Fred Hemmings has focused his attention to the bottom turning characteristics of the board".

Yeah, right. But lest anyone think Kimo McVay was taking surfing for a ride, it should be pointed out that Duke Kahanamoku loved the whole damn thing. He loved posing for all the press photos in his standard white outfit and red lei, he loved the big parties at the nightclub and he loved hanging out with the surfers. On the occasion of his seventy-fifth birthday, Kimo invited all the surfers to a big luau at the club, and when Duke arrived, he presented him with a Rolls Royce Silver Cloud with a big Duke meet trophy attached to the hood. Duke sat in the driver's seat, smiling and shaking his head. He didn't know how to drive, but McVay had a driver on call whenever he wanted to go somewhere. Duke Kahanamoku spent the last years of his incredible life being chauffered around Honolulu with a kind of bewildered grin on his face.

Says Jeff: "I guess I got about as close as a seventeen-year-old kid can to an old man, and I loved Duke. He had a kind of simple manner, wouldn't say too much, but now and then he'd just crack you up with his sense of humour. And he had a very spiritual side too, a real aura. All these years later, I don't remember the substance of what he said, but I remember feeling good when I was around him. He was a very handsome man with a great physique, even at that age, and he always carried himself with dignity. I don't know what he really thought about all the marketing bullshit, but maybe he was happy that it made Kimo happy."

For his part, Jeff liked the whole team deal, but he really loved his charge card at Duke Kahanamoku's. It was good for one hundred dollars a month, and no matter how hard he tried, he couldn't spend that much. Soon after he'd joined the team, Jeff borrowed his father's car and took a girlfriend along to see the Don Ho supper show. Jeff was seventeen and looked fourteen, and the maitre d' couldn't believe he actually had a reservation. "Sonny, this is a nightclub", he explained.

"My name is Jeff Hakman. I'm sure if you go out back and check, everything will be fine."

The fellow stomped off. A few moments later he was back, all smiles and hand gestures. "I'm terribly sorry, Mr Hakman. My mistake. This way please and I know you'll have a wonderful evening. What about a complimentary mai tai to start you off?"

Soon it was, "Your usual table, Mr Hakman?" Jeff had the coolest teenage act in town, and he knew it.

In September the whole team flew to California for the United States Surfing Championships at Huntington Beach. None of them did very well in the contest, which was won by David Nuuhiwa, but Jeff won the Duke Kahanamoku Sportsmanship Award, which was presented to Jeff by Duke himself. Back at the hotel, Kimo gathered them all in the bar. "Hey, I've got a great idea. We're goin' to Vegas, my treat. Duke wants to play the tables, so we're all gonna play the tables."

They flew to Las Vegas and checked into rooms at Caesar's Palace. Jeff and Jock Sutherland had rooms next to Duke's. After an initial session at the blackjack tables (Duke lost) Jeff was lazing around on the bed when the phone rang. It was Kimo. "Hey, Jeff, you guys need an education in fun. My treat. I'm sendin' some fun up for you both."

A few minutes later Jeff answered the knock on the door and let an attractive brunette in. There was an awkward period, but the girl, about six or eight years older than him, soon made Jeff feel at ease. When they had finished the hooker said: "Any other potential clients?"

Jeff said: "Oh yeah, my friend is in the next room. He's a little older, but he's a neat guy". The girl dressed, kissed Jeff lightly on the cheek and left. He heard the faint knock on Duke's door.

Jeff hadn't even begun to visualise the encounter in the next room when he heard doors slamming and the hooker burst back into his room. She was breathless and angry.

"You guys are sick, you know that? That's an old man in there, and I ain't bein' responsible for no heart attack." She slammed the door and was gone. When Jeff saw Duke later down at the tables, he looked a little bewildered.

If the inaugural Duke Kahanamoku Invitational had shown the surfing world a little about showmanship and razzmatazz, the 1966 World Surfing Titles in San Diego took the lesson a step further. In California, surfing would never get any bigger than it was that fall. The surf craze which had been building towards a climax since about 1963 was ready to burst, with surf shops on every corner and a zillion different superstar model surfboards being rammed down the throats of a willing but waning market. It was the year of the noserider, it was the year of David.

"David" was David Nuuhiwa, Hawaiian-born, California-raised from his early teens. He had a graceful, cat-like body-english and an incredible natural ability. He was the essence of cool. No one in California was in any doubt that Nuuhiwa would be the next world champion, and that the event in San Diego was merely a formality. No one, that is, except a small group of Australian surfers ensconced at the Santa Barbara home of kneeboarder and photographer George Greenough, and surfing early season Rincon and The Ranch at every opportunity. Head honcho in this little pack was Robert "Nat" Young, second in the world titles the previous year and determined to do better.

When the national and regional teams checked into their hotels on Shelter Island and took delivery of their team 1967 Chevy Camaros, the world contest had come down to a grand battle between the two Goliaths, David and Nat. The Hawaiian team included Paul Strauch, Ben Aipa, Jackie Eberle, Steve Bigler, Butch Van Artsdalen, Jimmy Lucas and, of course, Jeff Hakman, who had just been nominated by *International Surfing* magazine as the "best specialist big wave rider in the world". Since there weren't likely to be too many big waves in San Diego, this wasn't much help, but the hype just added to the generally wild vibe of Shelter Island.

Says Jeff: "Socially, it was just incredible. There were wild parties every night, girls running up and down the corridors screaming, quite a bit of pot and LSD. The Peruvians were just out of control. Hector Vallarde and one of his buddies took their team Camaro onto the beach and gave it a thrashing, doing donuts around people and generally terrorising. The lifeguards chased them off the beach, then the police chased them to the 405 freeway before they caught them. But Hector was one smooth guy, he told them that in Peru it was normal to drive on the beach. No charges were laid."

When the contest began at Ocean Beach Pier, it soon became obvious that it would be a duel between two completely different approaches to wave riding, developed on opposite sides of the Pacific. The California cruise, best exemplified by the surfing of Nuuhiwa and acolytes like Dru Harrison, used the surfboard as a platform for manoeuvres, some of them quite spectacular, like Nuuhiwa's ten second nose rides. The Australian power style of Nat Young and Queensland surfer Peter Drouyn used the surfboard to attack the wave, riding in parts of it that had never before been utilised.

Says Jeff: "Nat was cranking his board, a nine feet four inch thing he called Sam, and doing roundhouse cutbacks like I'd never seen before. He'd just drive it out onto the shoulder, plant those big feet of his on the rail, and wind it back in. Drouyn used a lot of little turns to tuck into the best part of the wave all the time, very tight, very controlled. They were both riding the wave, not the board, and that made the difference."

Jeff reached the quarter finals but none of the Hawaiians fared very well in mushy, marginal surf for most of the week-long party. The Nuuhiwa/Young confrontation was averted when Nuuhiwa was eliminated early, Young emerged the world champion and the Californians went away to consider their position.

Jeff: "I think Nat's performance at San Diego in '66 really was a benchmark in world surfing. It was the last of the longboard contests, and seeing what Nat could do on a board that was basically a log, made us all realise what was possible if we had better equipment."

LeROY GRANNIS

World Titles in San Diego, 1966. Toes upon the nose not quite enough.

CHAPTER 11

Sunset, 1968.

In June 1967 Jeff, aged eighteen, graduated from Punahou School and prepared to enter Maunaolu Junior College on Maui.

Jeff hadn't been exactly a straight-A student at Punahou, but in 1967 there was no question about the future for healthy American males of that age. They were in college or they were in the army and off to Vietnam. Entry into Maunaolu Junior College was relatively easy, and it was the favoured college of surfers for its proximity to Honolua Bay and Maui's other fabled surf spots.

Before he went off to college, however, Jeff needed to spend a working summer to get enough money to see him through the school year. This wasn't terribly difficult. He still had his three-year contract with the Duke Kahanamoku Surf Team, despite indifferent showings during the 1966 Hawaiian winter contests, and he had been invited by the director of the Punahou School summer co-ed program, Dan Wallace, to join Paul Strauch in teaching surfing at Waikiki. (This turned out to be a ten-year job and one of Jeff's most treasured experiences in surfing.)

On top of all this, Harry Hakman had begun to worry about Jeff's future. Since winning the Duke eighteen months earlier, he had seemed to drift aimlessly, hanging out with surfers who were more interested in getting high than improving their surfing. Neither Harry nor Jeff believed that there was any real prospect of a career in surfing, but Jeff had shown no interest in pursuing any other kind of career.

Harry took him aside one day and said: "Jeff, I've lined up a night job at Dole for you. You're not going to like it, it's hard work and the pay's lousy, but I want you to do it for a month, just for me."

If Harry had been expecting a battle over this, he was mistaken. Jeff thought about his father's challenge, and recalled all the previous challenges he'd placed before him. He hadn't much enjoyed going over the falls backwards at Palos Verdes Cove, but he felt it had made him a better and more dedicated surfer. He could handle whatever the Dole Corporation could dish out. He said: "Sure. When do I start?"

Jeff in power crouch to take the drop at Sunset.

Through June and July Jeff taught surfing from two to four each afternoon, then started at Dole at six in the evening and loaded pineapples into trucks until four in the morning. Then he'd fall into bed exhausted. Jeff recalls: "When the trucks arrived I'd have to climb up and open the gates and let the pineapples roll out, then get the hell out of the way or become pineapple crush! I got paid a buck fifty an hour, so it wasn't exactly a financial windfall, but Dad was impressed."

During the summer, Maunaolu College offered Jeff a sports scholarship. In return for surfing lessons, the college would pay for his accommodation off campus, so when he flew over to start the school year in September, Jeff set up house at Halehaku, near Hookipa Beach, with fellow Maunaolu freshman Jock Sutherland. The situation was perfect. Jeff and Jock bought a '57 Chevy, and with the house overlooking the Maui North Shore, they got a very early indication of a rising swell, and by driving a back way around the old port of Lahaina so as not to alert the surfer community there, they could get an hour or two of perfect Honolua Bay before the crowds arrived.

That fall something quite extraordinary began to happen on Maui. Some of the acid-head surfers were convinced it was the mystical power of Haleakala Crater at work, other less cosmic types thought that it was just a matter of being in the right place at the right time. But from September through into the spring of '68, Honolua Bay produced some of the biggest and best surf ever seen there, and for a brief point in time, this laidback rural oasis became the epicentre of the surfing world and the experimental laboratory for surfboard designs that would change the sport forever.

Jeff and Jock were new additions to a resident surfer community which already included Ryan Dotson, Les Potts and the enigmatic Hawaiian, Joseph "Buddy Boy" Kaohe. Then Dick Brewer moved over to shape in Lahaina for the winter, and teamed up with Buddy Boy to create Lahaina Surfing Designs which were built at John Thurston's factory in the Old Cannery. Jeff's buddy and Brewer team rider Gary Chapman followed Brewer over. Jackie Eberle came to stay with Jeff and Jock, then Gerry Lopez (a sophomore at University of Hawaii) and hot young Town surfer Reno Abellira arrived to get Brewer to shape them new boards. Then, in the same week, an Australian contingent arrived which included Nat Young, Bob McTavish, Russell Hughes, Ted Spencer and guru kneeboarder and wannabe Aussie George Greenough. Oh, and Jimi Hendrix was there too.

The exact sequence of events that fall and winter has been the source of conjecture and dispute for almost thirty years, and will probably remain so for another thirty years. Why? Because at Honolua Bay and the primitive shaping bays around Lahaina, the shortboard revolution began that season, and surfing performance rocketed into a new stratosphere.

In order to tell the story properly, it is necessary to backtrack just a little. Following the success of his "limited edition" concave guns for the Hobie label, Dick Brewer in 1966 moved on to the Bing label, for which he had produced a state of the art longboard he called The Pipeliner. These boards were nine feet six inches long, super thin and had minimal tail area. They turned beautifully on the face and were extremely responsive. Jeff had several Pipeliners between '66 and '67, and was riding one at Honolua Bay with considerable success when Gary Chapman arrived with a Brewer a foot shorter.

"What the hell is that?" he asked his friend.

"Try it", said Chapman.

Jeff surfed three or four waves on the shorter board and was sold. He recalls: "It was fantastic, it had tremendous acceleration and you could drive it from the nose. It was basically a scaled-down version of a standard gun, a pocket gun. I got Dick to make me an eight six with a green bottom and I rode it all season."

In a 1996 interview for this book, Dick Brewer said: "Jeff Hakman and Leslie Potts were the most creative surfers that year at Honolua Bay. The thing about Jeff was, like David Nuuhiwa and Gerry Lopez, he could take a new design and on the first day of surfing it take it to the limits of trimming and turning."

Jeff was back in Honolulu for a Duke promotion when Lopez arrived in Lahaina and pressured Brewer to start work on a board for him. According to an interview published in *The Surfer's Journal* in May 1992, Lopez wanted a nine feet eight board in the Pipeliner style, but before Brewer could start, the Australians arrived with their wide-tailed, vee-bottomed boards. According to Lopez: "John Thurston had a surf shop where all the boards got glassed, and (McTavish and Young) came there and we met 'em, and Brewer and McTavish kind of bullshitted for a long time. So the next day we go back to do my board and Brewer just takes the saw and cuts two feet off the blank, and it's eight six, and he tells me, 'That's how big a board you're getting!'"

Lopez's board was wider and more of a teardrop shape than the Chapman board, but clearly it worked for him. That winter saw the first photographs of the now-famous Lopez

JOHN WITZIG

Left: Buddy Boy Kaohe surfing deep at Honolua Bay, 1967.

Below: Reno Abellira with broken pocket rocket, and Betty Brewer, Honolua Bay, 1967.

JOHN WITZIG

lean into the barrel at big Pipeline. Rapidly, the test pilots of Honolua were spreading the word, but there is blood spilled in every revolution, even a shortboard one. In this case it was the blood of the Aussies.

Jeff was away for the entire swell that the contingent, led by Nat Young and McTavish, made their attack on Honolua. "When I got back I heard the story, or at least one version of it. The one I heard was that Chappy and the guys on the Brewer pocket rockets were surfing deeper and better than any of the Australians. It had nothing to do with their ability, it was simply that their equipment worked and the Australian boards didn't."

(The Australian *Surf International* magazine later made much of the alleged Australian invention of shortboard surfing in Hawaii that winter, prompting Brewer to write to the editor:"Hey, you guys, you're overlooking Chapman. The way I see it...Chapman's mini-gun pintail was a better trip than Nat's nine-four or Bob's nine-footer...Chapman's board was the breakthrough board.")

When Jeff flew back to Oahu a few weeks later for the Duke meet, he found that he was sharing a room at the Royal Hawaiian Hotel with Bob McTavish, the pint-sized and likeable surfer/shaper who normally eschewed contests. But McTavish was surfing in the Duke to prove a point. He told Jeff: "You don't need all that length to surf Sunset, you guys have got it all wrong". McTavish rode a nine feet four inch vee bottom in the eight to twelve feet surf and spent most of his heat swimming, but the photos of the event reveal some radical attempts at digging the big vee tail into the wall and turning vertically on the face, while the surfers who made the final (with the exception of winner Jock Sutherland and Jackie Eberle) played it safe.

Jeff made something of a comeback in this Duke, making the final and surfing consistently throughout, but it was Jackie Eberle who almost caused an upset in the best finish of his competitive career. Realising that he could not beat switch footer Sutherland on the rights, goofy footer Jackie went left and pulled off a couple of amazing rides before taking a swim that cost him the contest.

After the Duke, Jeff, Jock and Jackie headed back to the house at Halehaku and the continuation of the happening at Honolua. If the summer of '67 had been the summer of love on the West Coast, on Maui that year it was the winter of the purple haze. Acid rock guru Hendrix was in and out of town with his "Rainbow Bridge" film crew, at one stage putting

Bob McTavish power turns his vee bottom at Honolua, 1967.

Opposite: *Two views of Jeff at Sunset.*

on a concert for the stoned freaks hanging out in Haleakala Crater, and LSD was everywhere. Within the surfing community it was widely hailed as the wonder drug that could break down all inhibitions of mind and body, and allow the soul to roam free on nature's zippy-trippy, oh-so-beautiful waves of joy.

It was hard to get sensible conversation out of any surfers on Maui that winter, and the Hakman/Sutherland household was no exception. Someone was always passing through with a bunch of tabs, and the tripping became more and more frequent. There were plenty of funny scenes. The rented house at Halehaku was an old cane cutter's place with ancient fittings, including a rusty bathtub behind which an army of large rats liked to congregate. Jock's favourite sport was to pull a rat out from behind the bath, grab it by the tail and swing it from the balcony until the tail snapped. Since this could happen at any point in Jock's circular action, the rat frequently ended up splattering against an inside wall, or landing on whoever was crashed on the sofa. This cracked Jock up.

Says Jeff: "Jock could be a real pain in the ass. He was good at everything – great surfer, chess player, ping pong player, straight-A student. His mother was the same. She swam the Na Pali Coast by herself! We used to joke that the Sutherlands were from space, they just weren't human. But there was a serious side to Jock too. Like he wasn't at college to get

Jeff at Pipeline.

out of the draft, like all the rest of us. He felt he had a duty to serve his country and he was prepared to do that. But in the meantime he didn't mind having a little fun."

The surf crew used to congregate at the Pioneer Inn in Lahaina, or sometimes the Whale's Tail, but there was very little nightlife of interest on Maui, and the mindset of most of the surfers was that they had gone there to get closer to nature anyway. The generally approved method of getting closer to nature was to take lots of LSD and wander around the beaches and forests hallucinating.

As far as Jeff was concerned, the tripping was a pleasant adjunct to the surfing experience, but the two never became as one. He recalls: "I have some of the clearest and most beautiful surfing memories of my life from that year on Maui, those absolutely perfect days at Honolua, surfing with friends and watching their sillhouettes through the backs of the waves".

But for too many surfers, hallucinogenics became a way of life from which there was no turning back. One weekend Jackie Eberle disappeared while tripping and didn't reappear until the Monday evening. On Tuesday morning Jeff and Jock woke him before they left for school.

Jeff said: "There's not much swell, Jackie, but you're welcome to borrow the car and go look. You can just drop us off."

Eberle stared blankly at his friend. Jeff shook him. "Jackie, what's up? You okay?" Jackie Eberle wasn't okay. Jeff recalls: "We tried to bring him around but he'd tripped off to some place we couldn't get to, and he never came back. He was still sitting in the same position when we got home that day, and he never communicated properly with us again. Within a year he was in an institution.

"I made a vow that day to never again touch psychedelic drugs, and whatever other kind of fool I've been, I never have."

CHAPTER 12

In Jeff's last few months at Punahou School he had begun dating a senior called Sandy Raymond whose parents had a home in Lahaina, right in front of the Shark Pit left. When Jeff went to Maunaolu, Sandy followed, living at her parents' home and conducting an on-again, off-again romance. The romance was very much on when college broke for the summer, but while Jeff was back teaching surfing at Waikiki, Sandy announced that she was going to do her sophomore year at Cal Western in San Diego.

Jeff decided this time that he'd follow her. He arranged a transfer to Santa Barbara City College. Jeff and Sandy enjoyed a relationship that Jeff remembers as "hot and heavy", but never both at the same time. However there were also other reasons for him to move to California. For one, he was still freaked out about what had happened to Jackie Eberle, and he wanted to get away from the acid scene on Maui. For another, his three-year contract with the Duke Kahanamoku Surf Team expired towards the end of the year and several West Coast manufacturers had begun making overtures to him, among them Plastic Fantastic of Huntington Beach, who were also interested in putting his buddies Jock Sutherland and Gary Chapman on the payroll. Jeff figured if he was on the scene he could do the deals, plus living at Santa Barbara meant he would be certain of getting surf at Rincon.

But before he even finished the surf school in Honolulu, Jeff got a call from surfing filmmaker Curt Mastalka, who was shooting a new movie and wanted to base a large part of it around the surfing of Jeff and Jock Sutherland. Mastalka proposed two surf trips, the first to Stoner's Point in Mexico, the second across to the Gulf Coast and up the eastern seaboard. Jeff didn't know Mastalka too well, but it sounded like an adventure, and if Jock was going along, why not?

Mastalka had a campervan and Jeff and Jock slept in the back of it for most of the long trip to Stoner's. Mastalka had a few funny habits but the surf was good and Jeff and Jock were happy to do their job in the warm water. Then they piled back into the van and hit it to Santa Barbara.

Back on the mainland for college, Santa Barbara, 1968.

65

STEVE WILKINGS

Off The Wall, 1969.

The idea was to give Jeff a few days to organise accommodation for college, and for the moviemaker to process some test rolls and check the quality of his film stock. When they were ready to get started on the next leg, however, Mastalka made an announcement. Since they were heading in the general direction of across the Rockies and down through Texas anyway, he was going to detour slightly in order to visit his grandmother. In Nebraska. Perhaps because they were already asleep in the back of the van, or perhaps because geography had not been a strong suit for either of them, Jeff and Jock registered no protest.

Says Jeff: "After the first day of driving Jock and I started to figure we weren't headed for Texas, but Curt just kept going and going, and we kept getting closer to Canada. Finally we arrive at this place in Nebraska and it's bleak and overcast. Curt pulls up outside a little grandma type of house, and he goes and knocks on the door. He comes back in a while and he says there's no one home. So we leave Nebraska and we start driving in the opposite direction for the Gulf Coast. Jock and I just can't believe this. There's no one home? Didn't he call first?"

With the first stirrings of revolution in the camp, Mastalka and his team made for Port Isabel on the Texas coast, but by the time they got there, they had been fighting furiously for days over major issues like who would cook and who would wash up. The mood lifted briefly when they got good surf in Pensacola with local Gulf surfer Yancy Spencer, but not enough for Jeff, who jumped ship in Orlando and caught a flight back to California.

Mild-mannered Jock Sutherland continued on with Mastalka up the East Coast to New Jersey, where they left the coast and headed across country for California. Somewhere on the plains of the Mid-West, the van screeched to a halt and the moviemaker and his star got out and pummelled each other for fifteen minutes. Then they got back in the van and drove on in silence.

Jeff rented a house in Carpinteria, not far from Rincon, and settled into the college life. Actually, he settled in around the college life, taking virtually no part in it. He was way too busy. During the week he surfed Rincon whenever it was good, often in the company of George Greenough, and made occasional trips to The Ranch. Weekends he'd drive three hours to San Diego to hang out with Sandy. Life was pretty good, but Jeff felt he was marking time, that there had to be something better.

Just after Jeff's twentieth birthday in November, a college friend named Monty Smith told him he was planning a surf trip to Panama where he'd heard there was good surf. Was Jeff interested in coming? Hey, why the hell not? He felt a little bummed that he'd missed out on the world titles in Puerto Rico through not being available for selection in the Hawaiian team, so an adventure in Panama would be a good consolation. There was one small problem – Monty wanted to stay away for a couple of months. Jeff figured it wouldn't hurt to miss one semester of school, so he didn't register for the first semester of 1969.

He and Monty bumped on down the Pan American Highway just after Christmas and found warm water, waves and women, not to mention good, cheap dope and lots of it. Monty had a friend who lived in the Canal Zone, so they based themselves there while they made sorties to surf spots up and down the coast. One day on their return to the friend's home there was an urgent message for Jeff to phone his grandmother in Inglewood. All kinds of thoughts went through Jeff's head as he dialled the number, but none of them were as bad as the reality.

"Jeff, I don't know what to make of this but I've got a letter from the Draft Board. They want you to report for a medical immediately. They say you're no longer exempt."

This was Jeff's worst nightmare. His school had obviously informed the Draft Board that he hadn't re-registered. He left Monty Smith in Panama and flew back to face the music. Like most young American men in the late 1960s, Jeff had played through in his mind the idea of going into the army, of fighting in Vietnam. He had seen the bombings and the body bags on the TV news often enough, and he had friends in Hawaii who had survived the tour. "Don't go", they all said, and they all had that look of irretrievable sadness, like the war had robbed them of some part of their being, even if it hadn't taken their lives. Jeff had talked about the war with Jock, and Jock's willingness to go was something Jeff could never understand in his friend. It was like, if Uncle Sam says go, you go. Simple. It was simple for Jeff too. If Uncle Sam said go, you fought it with every last ounce of strength you had.

While he waited for his appearance before the Los Angeles Draft Board, Jeff, ever the optimist, began moving his things to Huntington Beach for his new job with Plastic Fantastic. He also began reading over the little dossier he had been putting together since his senior year at Punahou. The word around the schools at that time was start building your case early, and Jeff had gathered letters from several doctors outlining a history of stomach ulcers and a hereditary spinal condition which limited his movement. It wasn't much, but it was something, and Jeff clutched it to his chest as he walked, slightly unsteadily, to his physical.

The reason for his unsteadiness was that he had just downed an economy size tube of Crest toothpaste with six glasses of warm water, and the dry peppermint was threatening to choke him before it could lift his blood pressure to intolerable heights.

The medical evaluation hall at the Los Angeles Draft Board was a large and intimidating place, filled with people who were determined to prove that they were unfit for military service, and drill sergeant doctors who were equally determined to prove that they were. The people being tested had to follow blue lines on the floor until they were herded into cubicles for a series of physical and psychological tests. Jeff passed the hearing test with flying colours and moved through to other tests.

At one of the testing areas, the doctor beamed with recognition. "Hey, you're Jeff Hakman! How you doin', man? I remember you surfin' Makaha when you were real small. You were the toughest, strongest little guy..."

Jeff's heart sank. He clutched his dossier and moved on. Eventually he reached a check point where he was allowed to present evidence in relation to his health. Jeff briefly outlined his chronic problems and handed over the file. The doctor threw it to one side without looking at it. Well, that was that. Jeff didn't know whether to scream or cry, and there were plenty of guys doing both. But then the doctor ran through his check sheet, reached over and grabbed the discarded file. He quickly scanned the letters, then looked at the check list again. He said: "Must be some mistake. Go get your your blood pressure checked again."

Jeff realised he wouldn't get another chance. He prayed that the tube of Crest would kick in and peak at the right time. With a new test result he headed back to the evaluation tables, but this time he was herded to a different one. The doctor took only moments to reach a conclusion. He said: "Your blood pressure is high, very high in fact. Any idea why that might be?"

Jeff shook his head and the doctor sighed mightily. "You have two choices. You can stay at this facility for three days while we conduct further tests, or you can leave and have your own doctor conduct the tests and submit the results within a week."

Jeff couldn't believe it. This was a choice? "I'll get my own doctor to test me."

As he drove down the freeway to Huntington, Jeff had to pull over, open the door and throw up. It was probably relief, but it looked a lot like toothpaste.

Huntington Beach was full of surfers who knew about draft evasion. Jeff didn't have to look far to find someone who knew someone who knew a helpful doctor. He was given a business card with the name "Dr Filmore Testa" on it and a downtown Los Angeles address. This had to be some kind of little drug joke, since Bill Graham's Filmore Theatre concerts in San Francisco were then the home of the psychedelic acid rock movement. But Jeff dialled the number anyway and made an appointment.

Dr Testa was a nothing kind of guy in a nothing kind of downtown building. Jeff mentioned the name of his contact and asked to have his blood pressure checked. The doctor said: "Three hundred bucks. Cash." He held out his hand and Jeff filled it with money. Jeff didn't rate him highly for bedside manner but he wrote a good blood pressure report.

Three nail-biting weeks after he'd sent Dr Testa's report to the Draft Board, Jeff received his classification by registered post. He ripped open the letter. He was "1 Y" – required only in a national emergency. It wasn't a 4F (unfit for any military service) but it would do.

He danced around his little apartment. "Doc Testa, you money suckin' prick, I love your greedy ass!"

CHAPTER 13

Plastic Fantastic Surfboards was the 1968 brainchild of California surfers Dave Garner and Dan Callahan, a groovy, now label designed to capitalise on the shortboard revolution's fixation with design detail and psychedelic imagery. Every manufacturer on the West Coast was doing the same thing – even the straights who thought Lucy In The Sky With Diamonds and Puff The Magic Dragon were kids' songs – but by the summer of '69 Plastic Fantastic had arguably the biggest and best surfer design team around.

Why? The allure of drugs.

A full page magazine advertisement for the company shows Jeff looking down the foil from darkly-lidded eyes. The caption reads: "A Plastic Fantastic Stick is so-o-o good it will boggle your brain – Jeff Hakman."

The boys in the Huntington underground must have got a big giggle out of that one, since unbeknowns to Garner and Callahan, Plastic Fantastic chambered balsa boards filled with blond Lebanese hashish were being smuggled into California from Beirut via Mexico almost every other week. Drug deals were an open secret in certain echelons of the surfing industry, and were considered only marginally criminal even by those who didn't approve. It was a time of youth revolution, of overturning the system and being free, and in the minds of many in the surfing community, smuggling cash crops from Third World countries and selling them at a couple of thousand per cent mark-up to people who couldn't afford them was a significant political statement.

Jeff didn't think too much about any of that. PF was just a cool place to hang, the boards were good, there was cocaine to sniff at some of the more avant garde parties, he didn't have to go in the army, he didn't have to go to college, his buds were all there...It was 1969. As the period's best surf chronicler Drew Kampion put it in his definitive 1993 retrospective for *The Surfer's Journal*: "It was the best of times, it was the weirdest of times. Shit, it was the best of times."

That summer the Plastic Fantastic team included Gary Chapman, Jock Sutherland, Bill

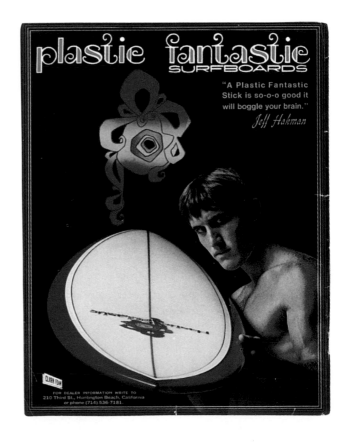

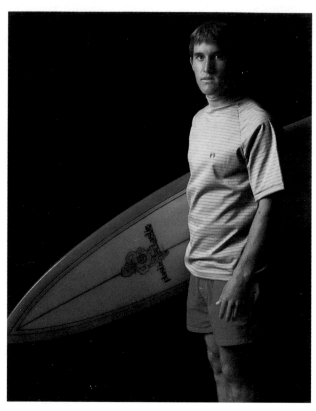

Publicity shot for Hang Ten, 1969.

Fury and Greg Tucker, as well as cleancut ace shaper Bruce Jones. Most of the boards were around the seven feet mark and roundtails (although Jeff had a six-four built by Dennis Choate for a promotions trip back East) and Jock Sutherland rode them better than anyone. Says Jeff: "In my view Jock peaked that year. He was the best surfer in the world. He wasn't as smooth as Nuuhiwa, but he could do anything on any wave. He was just remarkable."

Jeff shared a house with several of the Plastic Fantastic team members. One day he noticed a Volkswagen Kombi parked in the garage. The sliding door was pulled shut and a couple of his room mates were helping one of the leading shapers of the day pull plastic tubes of hashish out of the vehicle's every orifice. Jeff was amazed, the stuff was packed in everywhere. The shaper looked up at him and said: "Don't just stand there, give us a hand!"

Jeff also noticed that Greg Tucker was having a lot of balsa boards built, and yet he never saw him ride one and they never appeared in the Plastic Fantastic shop. One day Tucker and another surfer approached Jeff and Gary Chapman with a deal. They, Tucker and his friend, would bring some loaded boards in through Mexico City and drive them up to Baja. All Jeff and Chappy had to do was drive their own car across the border, meet them at a surf spot, swap boards and drive home.

Jeff was a little confused. "If you've already smuggled the stuff through customs in Mexico City, why don't you just drive them over the border at Tijuana too?"

"Mexico City's a cakewalk. They're getting to know us at Tijuana."

Jeff and Gary thought it over for a couple of days. There was five hundred bucks apiece in it for them, Gary reminded Jeff. Or a long stretch in jail, Jeff reminded Gary.

Jeff recalls: "Frankly, I was scared. Gary may have been too, but he didn't show it. He was just kind of shrugging and saying it sounded pretty easy to him. The next thing I know we're surfing down in Baja and Greg and his bud show up with the boards. It wasn't exactly a dramatic rendezvous. We just strapped the boards onto the car and hit it.

"We drove on up to the border and there were about ten lanes operating, with a long queue of cars waiting to go through the check points. It was kind of warm and we were just sitting, idling in the car, wearing boardshorts and tee-shirts. Gary was driving, I was shotgun. I started to think I could smell hashish, not very strong at first, just a little whiff. I tried to talk myself out of it, because obviously I was just experiencing fear, the realisation of what we were doing. But it got stronger. I asked Gary if he could smell it. He just kind of laughed and said no way. We were about four cars away from the check point when Gary's whole demeanour changed."

"Jeff, I think I can smell something too."

"Oh, shit! What're we gonna do?"

"Just stay cool, man. We can do this."

When they reached the check point the border guard smiled. "Any waves, guys?"

Gary said: "Not too many, nice day though".

"Sure is if you're not workin'. What you guys do?"

"Students."

"Cal West," Jeff chimed in, surprising himself with the confident timbre of his voice. He named a frat house he knew from his weekends with Sandy.

"Okay, guys, have a nice day." The guard waved them through.

Jeff's heart was still pounding when they pulled into a siding at Chula Vista and got out to examine the boards. "Jesus fucking Christ, man! Will ya lookit this!" One of the boards had been dropped on its tail in transit, cracking the fibreglass coating of the chambered stringer. In the heat of the day the hashish had begun to seep out and splash all over the back of the car. At a glance it looked like they had driven through a puddle. At a sniff it looked very much like they were going to jail.

They cleaned the hashish away with a beach towel, then put the offending board inside the car for the drive-by secondary check at Camp Pendleton. Much relieved and a grand richer, they celebrated that night with a few beers and a joint they scraped off the towel.

Following the success of the Baja run, Gary and Jeff were approached to do the full scam, bringing the hashish from its source all the way to home base at Huntington. Chappy was keen, and Jeff conveniently forgot about his pounding heart at the Mexican border. He was twenty years old, and if he pulled this one off he'd never have to worry about money again in his surfing career. Yes, they were in.

The plan was simple. Too simple. The backers put up five thousand dollars for all expenses and the split would be down the middle. All Jeff and Gary had to do was find a guy with no name in the Lebanese hash fields, buy a shitload of the stuff, pack it into the boards and bring it home through two customs searches. Such was their naivety that neither of the surfers even considered they were at serious risk. Hell, everyone was doing it!

They flew to London, then connected to Beirut. The customs officials at Beirut airport were reluctant to let them bring their surfboards into the country, but Jeff and Gary produced surfing magazines, showed their photographs and explained they were professional surfers. They checked into a downtown hotel, then also rented a nearby apartment for a week where they stashed the boards.

The following morning they rented a Volkswagen bug and, following the directions they had been given, took off across the top of Beirut and into the mountains, arriving mid-afternoon after a two hour drive. But arriving where? They had no map; they just studied the directions they had been given and eventually found the side road matching their description. Jeff spotted a little white house in the distance and Gary drove for it, but before they reached their landmark, a man about thirty five or forty stepped out in front of them, blocking the road. But he wasn't their man. The only thing they knew about their man was that he was just a kid, and this wasn't him.

"Hello, where do you go?" He spoke faltering English.

Gary mumbled something about them being lost tourists. Jeff laughed nervously.

"You are here to buy hashish?"

Gary looked over to Jeff, who shrugged. Gary said: "Maybe".

They followed the man to a house and were shown inside. They sat down at rickety chairs in an unadorned room and a Lebanese woman brought them tea. Another man appeared, then another. Eventually the first man asked: "How much you want to buy?"

"Forty kilos."

He nodded, spoke in Lebanese to the other men and they scurried off, returning soon after with a large bag of hash. The man said: "Now, you must pay good price..." He had barely started his sales rave when the door burst open and another man started yelling in Lebanese. The hashish disappeared instantly, the first man put a finger over his lips to indicate silence, and more tea was poured as yet another group of men walked in.

The atmosphere was suddenly electric. Jeff knew there was trouble, but who were all these guys? Then one of them spoke in perfect English. Jeff realised he was no more than sixteen or seventeen years old. He was their man! He said: "What are you doing here?"

Jeff said: "Just tourists, took the wrong road, got lost".

"You had better leave here right now, do you understand? This is a very dangerous place."

"Yes, we understand. We'll leave right now."

Jeff and Gary rose to leave and the young man and his attendants walked through the door and into the dusty courtyard with them. Then, as both groups got into their cars, the first man whispered to Gary: "Here at midnight". Gary nodded and drove off.

They drove back into Beirut to give themselves time to think. Was it dangerous, or just some little farmers' game designed to frighten off flakes? No one had a uniform, no one had a gun...the further away from the little pantomime they got, the more harmless it seemed. They knew this much: the first guy had the dope. They'd seen it. He wanted to sell it and he'd told them when to come back. The rest was bullshit.

Cleancut Jeff with Plastic Fantastic team-mate Bill Fury.

They ate a light meal and drove back. At midnight they drove down the same dirt road through the fields. The first man was waiting alongside a stone sleepout. He indicated that they had to drive somewhere else, and Jeff piled into the backseat to let him in. Gary drove on for half a mile until the man signalled for him to stop where two stone walls intersected at another stone building.

As Gary stopped the car a group of men charged from behind the wall and pulled the man bodily through the window of the small car. They were shouting and screaming and Jeff sensed real panic. The group of men pulled the first man over to the darkness of the stone walls. Jeff felt his heart in the back of his throat. More angry voices. Then a shot rang out, and another.

No one was paying any attention to the Americans in the car. Somehow Jeff was into the front seat head first and Gary had killed the lights and taken off. With his head down near the gear shift, Jeff cried out: "Hit it Chappy! They shot that fuckin' guy!"

They thumped down the track in the black night, their hearts pounding, and only dared to navigate with lights when they were a long way from the scene of the terror. They worked their way back across the paddocks in a wide arc, and eventually found the major road leading back towards Beirut. Shaking with fear, they drove all the way back into the city without stopping.

Jeff recalls: "To this day I don't know what happened against that wall, and I sure as hell didn't want to hang around to find out. But it seems to me they must have killed him. I don't think it was some kind of warning. I think he'd had his warning. My guess is that the first guy was trying to work around the syndicate, and he paid the price."

They sat in the hotel room in Beirut and slugged some calming whisky. What to do now? As the alcohol had the desired effect, they began to work through their problem logically. Neither was ready to give up and go home, but they could not go back up the lane, particularly not if they'd been witnesses to a murder.

Back in Huntington Beach they'd heard about a village called Ba'labakk, further into the mountains, where it was said that every second man on the street was a hashish dealer. You took a gamble on quality, but large purchases could be made. There was a military check point of some sort just outside of town, but it was never a bother. They decided to drive up and take a look the next day.

Says Jeff: " We drove straight through the check point and Ba'labakk turned out to be this sleazy little town with dirty, cobblestone streets and kids and animals running everywhere. We drove around for a little while – a real little while – and this guy jumped onto the running board and started jabbering about hashish. A nod was all it took. He led us up a laneway and into a walled compound, where we pulled up and he took us into a living room where he'd set up a little office. He spoke quite good English and he was businesslike, so we thought maybe this would be okay."

The seller asked: "How much do you want?"

"Forty kilos."

The seller nodded and made a phone call. He put down the phone, told them the price and that the hashish would be delivered within forty-five minutes. Jeff smiled the thinnest of smiles. Even the price wasn't too bad, considering the alternatives they had left. The seller reached into a desk drawer and pulled out a photo album. He opened it at a page full of snapshots of himself with young people who looked much like Jeff and Gary.

"This is my friend Artie from Hermosa Beach, California. He come three times, buy fifty kilo each visit. Good business. This is Kevin from Houston, Texas. Very important man in that city. He buy one hundred kilo. This is..." He went on through the album as the minutes passed too slowly. Jeff wondered what he would say if asked to pose for a snapshot, but neither he nor Gary was asked.

Eventually a man arrived with the hashish. They sniffed the open bag and told their new friend they'd trust him for the weight. The delivery boy helped them load it into the bug's front trunk, they paid the seller, thanked him profusely and drove out of the compound in a state of great relief. So what if they'd paid over the odds? So what if they were a couple of kilos light? There would still be a good profit for everyone.

They hadn't gone five hundred yards when another Lebanese jumped onto the running board and spoke urgently. "The police know you have the hashish and they will stop you at the check point. You will never make it, but I can help you."

Gary pulled up at the kerb and looked at Jeff. "Fuck, man, this is just a sting. This is total bullshit!"

"Yeah, Gary, but what if it isn't?"

The man on the running board was making loud noises. "Not bullshit, not bullshit. I tell you the truth."

Jeff recalls: "I think Gary and I both knew the guy was lying, but how far was he going to take it? If we didn't play his game, maybe one phone call is all it takes and we're in some scummy jail for the rest of our lives. We weren't prepared to take the risk."

Gary said: "Okay, you win".

They were led to another house where the hashish was unloaded and stashed in a shed. It would be delivered safely to them in Beirut within twenty-four hours. They would pay five hundred American dollars on delivery for this very good service.

Jeff and Gary drove back into Beirut, emotionally exhausted. They waited forty-eight hours, but, of course, the courier didn't come. Enough was enough. They scouted the city area for a suitably accessible vacant block, then bought two shovels at a hardware store. Late at night they dug a hole and buried the surfboards. In the morning they flew to London and rerouted their return tickets to Los Angeles instead of Mexico City.

There was no homecoming celebration this time. They simply went to see the money men to break the bad news.

"Jesus, am I glad to see you guys! We've been worried out of our minds. Nixon has done a deal with the Mexicans over Operation Intercept and there have been four busts there in a week. You don't know how lucky you are."

"Yes, we do," Jeff said under his breath.

CHAPTER 14

Hamming it up as a sleazeball.

The balls-up in Beirut made a neat hole in the middle of summer, and by the time Jeff had started to put it behind him, it was almost fall. He was just starting to make plans for a possible winter on the North Shore, promoting Plastic Fantastic and catching some waves, when he received another letter from the Draft Board, telling him to report for a second physical in just under a month's time.

Jeff went into shock. Uncle Sam wasn't going to take no for an answer. Shit, Jock wanted to go, for Christ's sake! Take Jock and leave me alone!

He asked around. Yeah, this looked bad. There was Canada, of course, and some dudes were hiding out down in Cabo, or Panama better yet. Or there were other ways.

"Like what?" Jeff asked his contacts in desperation.

"There are three ways that are proven, Jeff, but you gotta be good. Fuckin' good, because these guys have seen everything. Okay, there's space case. You go live in a cave for a month and take LSD every day, you don't change your clothes, you don't wash. When you go for the physical you put rocks in your pockets and you shit your pants while you're in there, and act like nothin' happened. That's space case."

It sounded ugly but Jeff's surfing friend Mike Turkington had done space case in Hawaii and pulled it off.

"Next there's junkie. Get yourself a habit real quick. Walk in there loaded to the eyeballs and dump all your syringes and shit on the table right in front of them. That's junkie."

Junkie sounded horrible. Jeff didn't want to do that.

"And then there's faggot. Jeff, you don't want to do faggot. It wouldn't work."

While Jeff considered his options he also sought a change of venue, believing that the evaluating doctors in Hawaii might be less world weary than their Los Angeles counterparts. He wrote to the Draft Board, telling them that he was relocating to Hawaii for work and requesting a transfer of his test. He was told to report at Fort De Russy in six weeks time.

Soon after his return to Hawaii, he was explaining to a North Shore friend his intention to do space case. The friend said: "Jeff, there is nothing in army regulations that says you can't shit in your pants. There is something that says you cannot be homosexual."

Jeff was sold. He went to see his sister Jeannine and pleaded with her to turn him into a homosexual. She thought this was hilarious, but Jeff grabbed her by the forearms and said: "Jeannine, I've never been more serious about anything in my life. Make me queer!"

The lessons started the next day. Jeannine taught him how to walk with a subtle hint of femininity, like someone trying to disguise it. She shaved him all over and suggested he grow his hair a little longer so she could tease it. At night Jeff started going to transvestite bars in Honolulu, picking up helpful hints.

Jeff recalls: "I was very serious about the whole deal. I mean my future was at stake. I did my homework every day, memorised little turns of phrase, and gay mannerisms. It was very much a scientific preparation."

On the morning of the test Jeff was up at dawn. Jeannine and another friend who had done faggot and beaten the draft helped him prepare. He was smooth shaven all over and Jeannine lightly made him up and teased his hair, paying close attention to the little curls in his sideburns. He wore a vee-neck blouse of his sister's, tight, tight denim shorts frayed and cut very high, and slipper style shoes with slightly raised heels.

Jeff parked about two hundred yards from the main gate and concentrated on his walk as he made his way to the evaluation. A group of men wolf-whistled as he passed. Yes! thought Jeff, looking good. After the episode in LA, the thing he feared most was recognition, and it happened almost the moment he walked in.

"Jeff, is that you? Jeff Hakman?"

He was a surfer from Haleiwa. Jeff brushed straight past him without making eye contact. Compared to Los Angeles, the Honolulu evaluation was positively mellow. About forty men sat in a central hall and filled in a medical form. When Jeff got to the question about homosexuality, he wrote "NO" in bold letters. One by one the men were called into various examination rooms. Jeff was called in, put through some basic physical tests, then sent elsewhere for psychological testing.

The psychologist looked at him for a very long time before asking a question. Then he said: "Mr Hakman, do you want to go into the service?"

Jeff ran a manicured finger over his bottom lip, as though applying lipstick. he replied: "Yes, I do".

"And why would that be?"

Jeff played his trump. He tried to look seductive and shy at the same time. "Well, I don't have many friends. I guess I'm kind of lonely and I think I might meet some new friends in the service."

The psychologist pushed Jeff's medical form back across the desk. "Have another look at that, son. Is there anything you haven't told us?"

Jeff pushed the form back across the desk and studied his nails. "No sir, there's not."

There was a mighty sigh and Jeff was dismissed. Three days before his twenty-first birthday he received his 4F in the mail.

The invitations to the fifth annual Duke Kahanamoku Invitational were out and Jeff hadn't received one. He was in good company. Nat Young, Wayne Lynch, David Nuuhiwa, Steve Bigler and Barry Kanaiaupuni hadn't received one either. Of course Jeff probably didn't deserve one, regardless of how the polling worked. Since his inaugural win, he hadn't exactly covered himself with glory in the event, and in 1968 he bombed out in his heat.

But he nursed just a little bit of hurt. He retreated to the North Shore house he was sharing with Ryan Dotson and mapped out his future as a soul surfer and adventurer. In fact he was just about to phone Maui for a surf check when Buddy Boy Kaohe called him.

"Hey Jeff, come on over man. The bay's gonna pump next few days. Nobody here yet, too early in da season, huh. You come over, Jeff and I gotta see you 'bout sumpin' too."

Jeff flew over and caught the first good swell of what was to be a vintage winter, the best in living memory. The first evening Buddy Boy took him aside for a couple of beers. Jeff liked Buddy Boy – he had such a sunny, open nature that everyone did. But he also had a dark side, seen only by those with whom he had close dealings. Deep below the surface, Buddy Boy was a plotter and a conniver, and eventually it would be his undoing.

He told Jeff he had a plan. He'd heard about him and Chapman, crazy sonsabitches. Nothing like that, this was a good plan. Jeff listened. They would pool funds and fly to Thailand, where Buddy Boy just knew they could score high grade weed. There was a United States military base just near Pattaya Beach and Buddy Boy had heard they allowed American expatriates to use their postage and freight facilities. Was anyone gonna suspect a shitload of dope coming out of a US military base?

Jeff thought it sounded good, maybe lacking in a little detail. He and Buddy Boy shook on it. Within a week they were in Bangkok.

Jeff said: "What's the plan, Bud?"

"There is no plan. Let's go get a drink."

In a bar off Patpong Road they struck up a conversation with some Thai students. Buddy Boy was good like that. He had that Hawaiian way, people wanted to befriend him. Eventually they all went to a nearby flat shared by the students and smoked a joint.

Buddy Boy said: "Man, this is good shit. I'd like to buy some like this."

A young man, tall by Thai standards, became the broker of the deal. "How much you want?"

"Depends on price. Maybe one hundred kilos."

The students went into a huddle.

"Yes, this is possible, but it will take some time to organise. Maybe one week."

Jeff and Buddy Boy arranged to meet the students in the same bar in a week's time, rented a car and drove down to Pattaya Beach. On the way they stopped at a department store cum warehouse in the suburbs and bought some large, cheap hi fi speaker boxes, plus some packing materials. The speakers were Buddy Boy's idea too, but Jeff thought this made a lot of sense. Everyone knew hi fi equipment was cheap in Asia, and it was a logical thing for a young serviceman to send home.

They rented a house on the beach and chilled out for a week, staying high on the dope sample they'd been given. Back in Bangkok they met up with the students and drove with them upcountry for several hours. It was a pleasant enough trip through the terraced rice fields to the River Kwai, and when they arrived at their destination they were shown to a little cafe and bar in the middle of nowhere. The farmers and landholders were brought, one by one, to meet the new customers, and finally the marijuana was produced and a price negotiated. Jeff and Buddy Boy then drove back to town in their car while the students stayed to organise the transportation. Well pleased with the business, they had a night on the town in Bangkok.

The next morning they drove to a house to take delivery. Buddy Boy opened one of the bags and was horrified to see the state of the weed, all sticks and clumps of dirt. He insisted that it be cleaned up, and the entire family of one of the students – three generations including a very old grandmother – got to work, shaking, cleaning, repacking. Eventually it was considered acceptable, loaded into the car and taken to Pattaya.

The plan seemed to be working pretty well, but there were still some kinks to be ironed out. For example, Buddy Boy knew that Americans could usually send parcels through the base mail, but he wasn't sure if it was stricly within regulations, nor how you went about finding out.

One night Buddy Boy struck up a conversation in a bar with a cleancut, expensively-dressed American. He was a surfer and he wanted to know all about Maui. Jeff asked him where he worked.

"I'm the manager of the Chase Manhattan Bank over at the base."

Buddy Boy was in like a shot.

"Man, maybe you're the answer to our prayers. We bought these stereo speakers – real high tech shit, you know – and we want to make sure they get back home in one piece. We heard the mail out of the base was the safest way to go."

"No problem, happy to help you out. Just let me know when you want to send 'em and I'll come round and organise it for you."

Jeff and Buddy Boy spent the next two days pulling the woofers out of speaker boxes, packing them with dope and jamming them back in again. They filled six speakers and still had a room full of weed.

Buddy Boy said: "I bet they don't even look twice at stuff coming from the base. Why don't we just pack the rest of it neatly in boxes?"

They filled four boxes and still had dope left over. The man from the bank was coming in the morning to help them despatch the speakers. They decided to dump the rest. In the middle of the night they crept down onto the beach at the outgoing tide and emptied several bags of top quality Thai into the sea.

Jeff said: "I never thought I'd see that". He watched as the light offshore breeze blew the contraband seaward.

Jeff was first up in the morning, stretching as he looked out over the sun-drenched sea. He noticed the white caps, felt the onshore wind in his face, then looked with horror at the marijuana strewn all over the beach at the high water mark. The wind had turned in the night and blown the stuff straight back onto the beach! It looked almost like seaweed. On the edge of panic, Jeff and Buddy Boy waited outside at their car until the bank manager arrived, so that he wouldn't see the mess on the beach. Then they drove in convoy to the base and posted the speakers. Buddy Boy had been right. No one gave them a second look. Satisfied that there was no rigid inspection, they made arrangements to post the rest of the boxes the following day, then drove back to Pattaya and checked out of the beach house, leaving the incriminating weed on the sand.

CHAPTER 15

Haleiwa, 1969.

A few days before Jeff got home, a swell of immense proportions hit the North Shore, peaking at around midnight on Monday, December 1. At Waimea forty feet waves closed out the bay and the tidal surge washed away dozens of houses, Dick Brewer's included. At Kaena Point waves of sixty feet or more went unridden, and at Makaha on the morning of Thursday, December 4, Greg Noll took off on an absolute monster, dropped smoothly to the bottom and bailed out. Experienced onlookers, Fred Hemmings among them, declared it the biggest wave ever ridden.

While all this was happening, Jeff Hakman and Buddy Boy Kaohe were stuffing marijuana into cardboard boxes in Thailand. Perhaps because he felt strange at having missed such an all time swell, or perhaps as some kind of anxiety therapy, Jeff began surfing all day, every day. Right through into the leadup to Christmas. Every morning he woke up thinking about those speaker boxes arriving at Haleiwa Post Office, and every morning they weren't there, he lost himself in his surfing. He may have been out of the Duke, but he was hot property on the North Shore. His timing and placement were perfect, he was fitter than ever, his boards were working and he seemed totally focused.

He wasn't, of course. Jeff would wake up in a sweat in the middle of the night. It was the guys in black suits at the door dream. "DEA, Mr Hakman, we have a warrant to search your house."

Then one day the boxes started arriving. Not the speakers, the smaller boxes. The ones they sent after the speaker boxes. "It's probably just because they're bigger or something," Jeff told Buddy Boy. They were addressed to a fictitious person at a friendly address, and Henry the postman just delivered them right to the door with the rest of the Christmas parcels. It seemed easy enough. Buddy Boy split for Maui with half the stuff, and Jeff started getting rid of pounds at six hundred bucks a pop.

There was a big seasonal demand, not just on the North Shore but all over the island, so for convenience and safety (more than one North Shore house had been burgled for

Above: Roundhouse cutback at Haleiwa, 1969.

Left: Jerry's Sweet Shop in old Haleiwa, a favourite hang.

Two views of Jeff as he approached his prime in 1970.
Above: at Pipe.

Right: jamming off the bottom at Pupukea.

dope) Jeff decided to stash some of the stuff at his parents' place in Honolulu. He borrowed a rusty old pickup with a canopy, shovelled forty pounds of dope into the back and covered it up, and set off into town. At Beretania he changed lanes without looking and ploughed into a brand new Chevy Impala.

Says Jeff: "I just knew this was bad trouble. The car was creased pretty bad and this Japanese guy gets out with his family. He has to crunch the doors open, and he's got his head in his hands, and he wants to call the cops. I'm telling him this really won't be necessary, because I'm a nice guy and I know it's entirely my fault. The guy wants to call the cops so bad, but I just keep pleading, and eventually he agrees to follow me up to my parents' house. I go get a wad of hundreds and I just keep peeling them off until he's happy. For all I know there was enough to buy a new Chevy, but the problem went away."

Because he didn't want to be seen hanging around the post office at Haleiwa, Jeff had done a deal with a friend to check out the inward parcels every day. (The speaker boxes were too big for mailman delivery.) Early in the new year the friend called.

"They're here."

"You sure."

"Pretty sure."

Jeff drove down into Haleiwa and sauntered into the post office with some fake letters to post. Behind the counter he could see the speaker boxes, all taped up and tied with yellow string. Yellow string? Jeff could have sworn they'd used red string. But he'd been imagining a lot of stuff lately. He put it out of his mind and drove out to his friend's house.

"It's them, all right. You want to pick 'em up and make a few bucks?"

The friend was in. He borrowed a truck (a different truck), picked up the speakers without any problems and delivered them to Jeff at Sunset Point. Together, they started stacking the boxes in the living room, but they could be seen from every window, and there seemed no place to hide them in the little walk-through bungalow.

Jeff said: "Wait, I don't like this. Let's take it all into town."

They loaded up the truck again and started driving the back way into Honolulu through Kahuku. As they passed the new Del Webb Kuilima Hotel complex, a black car tailgated them for a moment, then swung onto the wrong side of the Kam Highway and drew up alongside them. It was a black Cutlass and the guys in the front looked for all the world like cops. They signalled to Jeff to pull over and cut in ahead of him to ensure that he did. As the truck came to a halt, squad cars converged on the scene from both directions.

Jeff said: "Oh, shit!"

They were hauled out, stretched over the hood of the Cutlass, frisked and cuffed by officers with their guns drawn. It was like a bad movie. They were placed in two different cars, wedged between detectives.

The driver of the Cutlass said to Jeff: "Okay, asswipe, start talkin'."

Jeff and his buddy had rehearsed a little riff in case of emergency. It was entirely predictable but they hadn't really thought they'd have to use it. The dope wasn't theirs, a couple of guys had hired them to pick it up, didn't get their names, they'd get paid when they delivered to the car park at Kahuku in an hour's time.

The police formed a convoy with the truck in the middle, and they rolled on up to Kahuku. Jeff sat tight in the car park while the cops made themselves invisible.

"What're they gonna do to us when Mister Big doesn't show?" Jeff's friend asked.

"I guess he got tipped off," said Jeff. "Shit, plenty of people would have seen them nail us. Hey, it's the best we got."

The police gave it half an hour past time, then cuffed them again and hauled them off to Honolulu PD. Jeff and his friend were charged with possession with intent to sell, while the police conferred with their federal colleagues over a range of importation charges.

The next morning it was all over the papers, "Surf champion held on drug charges", and Jeff was all washed up or a hero, depending on where you stood on the recreational drug issue.

Haleiwa, 1970.

The case against Jeff was an extremely complex one, since it had emanated from the interception of the US Mail at a mainland receiving depot. There were strict laws governing the interception of mail under most circumstances, and the lawyer the Hakmans engaged, a sharp young former DA's assistant named Brook Hart, immediately began a full investigation into the legality of how the sting had been put together. Meanwhile, Jeff was out on bail and Buddy Boy had gone deeply underground.

Says Jeff: "My life was pretty much a mess in some ways. I mean it looked like I might have to go to jail, I was kind of a failure as a smuggler, my job with Plastic Fantastic was falling apart...the only thing I had left was surfing, and it just happened that I was starting to surf the best I would ever surf in my life. While all this shit was going down, I clung to that."

With three to five years hanging over his head and his name in the headlines for all the wrong reasons, Jeff Hakman's commercial value had slumped somewhat. Most businessmen would have run a mile from an association with him, but Duke Boyd was not most businessmen. Boyd had started the Hang Ten label in the early 1960s and built it up into surfing's first crossover label, a multi-million dollar business which put surf gear on the shelves that Middle America could reach at stores like Macy's and Liberty House.

Jeff had known Boyd a little for several years, but they got quite close in the summer of 1969 when Jeff and Gary Chapman would often hang out at Duke's house in Huntington

Beach. He was about fifteen years older than them, not quite athletic and not quite a surfer type, despite the fact that he was involved with his friend Dick Graham in publishing *Surfing* magazine. But Duke was funny and smart and he had a unique way of looking at things. Before Duke Kahanamoku died in 1967, Jeff had loved to listen to him talk, not so much for what he said, but the way he said it. This Duke was different. What he said demanded attention.

One evening in Huntington, Duke drew Jeff a little diagram and passed it across the table to him. It showed a little stick figure on a tiny surfboard doing aerial manoeuvres above the waves. Duke said: "This is what surfing will be like in the future".

Says Jeff: "He was dead right".

In 1969 Duke Boyd sold the Hang Ten label to the Richton Corporation for three and a half million dollars, bought a ranch and ski lodge in Woody Creek, Colorado, then set about starting a new label. One of the first people he contacted was Jeff Hakman.

Jeff recalls: "Duke had serious business partners in the new company, Golden Breed, and I'm sure he had to massage me into the deal a little bit. But he was smart enough to recognise that a label started in a boardroom by a bunch of millionaires didn't have what Hang Ten had when it started. Hang Ten grew out of the surf culture and that gave it credibility. Golden Breed had to buy into the surf culture, and they bought me."

On bail and unable to leave Hawaii, Jeff secured through Duke Boyd a clothing sponsorship from Golden Breed, a board sponsorship from Bing Surfboards and a three hundred dollar a month salary. He missed the 1970 world contest at Bells Beach in Australia (won by Californian Rolf Aurness) and kept a low profile out of the water. In the water was another matter. Throughout the summer he kept up the momentum, teaching surfing in town (despite some qualms from the Punahou School board), and surfing at Ala Moana and all over the South Shore breaks. As the winter season approached, he was in superb form.

The only thing that brought Jeff down that fall was bad news from his lawyer, so when he came home from surfing and got a message to call Brook Hart, he did so begrudgingly. Hart came on the line almost immediately.

"You're a free man, Jeff."

"Say what?"

"Free. Charges dismissed. You walk."

Jeff couldn't believe this, it had to be some sick joke. But sick jokes weren't Brook Hart's usual style. He explained that the mail intercept had been deemed illegal and any evidence emanating from it was therefore inadmissable. The feds had held up the delivery of the US Mail for a few hours too long and the whole case had fallen apart on a technicality. Somewhere in a government office, some one's butt would be getting kicked good and hard, but on the North Shore of Oahu, the world's worst smuggler was a very happy man.

LEROY GRANNIS

Above: *Classic cutback at Sunset.*

Left: *Haleiwa, 1970.*

LEROY GRANNIS

CHAPTER 16

Right: At Sunset in the 70s.

Opposite: The world's best contest surfer, 1971.

During the early fall of 1970, Duke Boyd phoned Jeff in Hawaii and invited him to spend a few days at his recently-acquired ranch in San Juan Capistrano to discuss an idea he had for a new kind of surfing contest. Dick Graham would be there, Duke said, and he was trying to get in touch with Gary Chapman.

Over a few days Duke outlined his plans to create a "core group" of North Shore surfers on the Golden Breed payroll, emphasising the label's commitment to surfing's "roots". This made a lot of sense to Jeff and Chappy, since surfing was going through an anti-establishment phase in which the value and validity of the contest system was continually being questioned. The magazines and movies were full of clichés about freedom, brotherhood and equality, while contests such as the Makaha International and the Duke seemed to be all about systems, regimentation and exalting one person above all others.

Tough-talking former GI Graham also weighed in with the observation that Golden Breed's number one frontman, Jeff, would be a highly unlikely inclusion in the Duke invitation list anyway, given his problems with the law.

Jeff replied: "If they invite me I'll win it".

Boyd turned the conversation back to his plan to identify Golden Breed with the tempo of the times. He said: "What we need to do is provide a focus for surfing performance that is not a surfing contest. No winners or losers, just performances."

"An expression session," Jeff said. Boyd and Graham both looked at him. Bingo!

The Golden Breed Expression Session was slotted to happen as the opening event on a crowded winter calendar, followed by the first Smirnoff Pro to be held in Hawaii, (the inaugural event had been held the previous year in California) the Duke and the Makaha International. With first place purses of two thousand dollars and one thousand dollars respectively, the Smirnoff and the Duke represented the birth of a professional North Shore tour. The Expression Session, on the other hand, offered every invitee a two hundred dollar appearance fee. Very democratic, very cool, and very welcome, since some surfers

Repeat after me, I'm an individual.

spent less than two hundred bucks (excluding dope) on the North Shore all winter, and many of them weren't actually going to win a contest.

While Boyd and Graham looked after the television coverage and the logistics of the whole affair, Jeff sat down to map out an invitation list. In surfing, the job of preparing an invitation list, then and now, is the equivalent of ritual disembowelment. No matter how you cut it, you are going to offend people. For this reason, Jeff's role was kept secret, although you didn't have to be Einstein to figure that Golden Breed's main man was going to have something to do with it. But had Jeff's role been spelled out at the time, it would surely have led to accusations of cronyism and even personal vendetta. (As it turned out, by the time the Expression Session invitations went out, Jeff had been invited to the Duke but not the Smirnoff.)

Jeff in fact thought long and hard about who he would invite to this experimental meet, realising that the credibility of his friend's new company rested very heavily on the outcome. The standard criticisms of the Duke invitation list were that it was made up of yesterday's heroes, that too many Hawaiians were included and that there was no allocation for "wildcards" or surfers who had made their reputations only in the preceding twelve months. Jeff tried to diffuse all of these negatives in his list and to include some "soul" surfers who never or rarely competed, but whose ability on the North Shore was legendary.

So he sat at the kitchen table of the little house he had just rented at Pipeline with student Mark Munro, and started writing names down. Nat Young was first, the best all-round surfer in the world. Barry Kanaiaupuni was next, awesome at Sunset, the quintessential North Shore power surfer, then at the peak of his powers. Jock, the best surfer of 1969 and now the best surfer in uniform. Keith Paull, power glider from Australia who shredded on the North Shore. Reno Abellira and Gerry Lopez, the new Brewer crew, both smooth and brilliant in different ways. Chappy, of course, and Chappy's little brother Owl, and Owl's buddy Sammy Hawk, new on the North Shore with a radical approach, Jackie Baxter, one of the best at Sunset...and so it went.

Jeff chose 19 surfers to join him for a two-week waiting period on the North Shore, from which the best day would be chosen to conduct a totally free-form event. The best surfers on the best waves, free to break through the performance barriers. And best of all, once the apparatus was in place, the organisers agreed that it was the surfers' call; they would decide when and where to hold the event.

In keeping with the informal, folksy and soulful nature of the Expression Session, Duke Boyd and Dick Graham decided to forego the usual formalities and launch proceedings with a barbeque on the beach. Or more correctly, at Jeff's new rented house right next to the beach. Just some beers, some burgers (tofu, of course) and some bullshit, make everybody feel welcome kind of thing. Duke sprung for the beers, Dick agreed to wear the chef's apron, and Jeff swept the sand and the roaches out of the little house. They called it the Good Karma Party.

Duke Boyd and Dick Graham arrived early with the beer and the food, and a sixty-something gentleman named Bob McAlister, who just happened to be the chairman of the Don Rancho Corporation, which was the manufacturer for both Hang Ten and Golden Breed. A smallish, wide-eyed fellow in a leisure suit and aloha shirt, Bob McAlister had never been to Hawaii before, and he was sure as hell looking forward to meeting these surfers.

The invitees started to drift in around four, and by five the house was filled with people and surf talk. David Nuuhiwa, all hair and Satanic presence, chatted in a corner with Duke Boyd and Greg Tucker, out back on the beach side, Herbie Fletcher and Ryan Dotson helped Dick marinate the steaks for those who hadn't paused to consider the slaughter of helpless animals.

"It was loose," Jeff recalls. "I was just boppin' round, makin' sure everyone was having fun, and, well, everyone was having fun."

The truck pulled off Kam Highway just on dark, about six, and rumbled straight on up the lane to Jeff's house on the beach. Jeff looked through the kitchen window just as its

Backdoor Pipeline, 1970.
Jeff's in-the-pocket placement was never better.

awesome cargo started to unload. It was a big truck and it was holding big men. Locals. In the thick of it were the Aikaus, legends on the North Shore, as much a part of the Hawaiian tradition as the ukelele players at Nanakuli, or a jug of swipe at Thanksgiving. Clyde was in the lead, Eddie behind him with the other brothers. Somewhere in back was Butch Van Artsdalen ("Mr Pipeline" of the early '60s and the acknowledged master of that break until Jock Sutherland and Gerry Lopez happened along, a high school blue from La Jolla, born in Norfolk, Virginia, in point of fact, but near enough a local now) and a half-dozen other drinkin' bro's from Haleiwa's Seaview Inn.

They were very drunk and very unhappy. They had spent the previous six hours lamenting the fact that Mr Pipeline had not received an invitation to the Expression Session. They might just as easily have lamented the fact that Eddie Aikau had not received an invitation either, but the subject of the beef was Butch. They lamented for a few hours in the Seaview, then they bought a few cases of Primo beer and sat over in the beach park and lamented some more. (In fact, the main reason Mr Pipeline hadn't been invited was that in recent years he had spent too much time lamenting and not enough surfing.)

Then some one had the bright idea that they should all drive up to Pipeline and share their views.

Mark Munro's dog Stanley started growling. Jeff went to the door to meet them.

"Hi, Clyde. What's happenin'?"

"We want to talk to Mr Graham."

"Dick? Oh, sure. Wait right here."

Jeff scampered through the house and down the steps, and found Dick Graham working the hibachi and deep in conversation. Jeff whispered to him: "Dick, someone to see you out front..." Before he could complete the message with any kind of subtlety, Graham had shot around the side of the house to see who it was. Jeff was about to follow after him when Gary Chapman appeared at the top of the steps.

"Jeff, quick! Come here."

Chappy pulled him out of earshot of the guests. "Man, this could get real ugly. These guys are fucked up and ready to burn someone. Any fucking one! We gotta get the old dude outta there!"

The boat! Jeff flashed on his neighbour's upturned dinghy down on the sand in front of the house. It was getting dark and Bob McAlister would be safe there until the trouble passed. Jeff wedged his way into the house, moving against a tide of people trying to get out as Clyde and the boys came busting through the front. He grabbed McAlister by the lapel of his leisure suit.

"Bob, look, it's getting a bit like the wild west in here. Maybe you should come with me."

McAlister didn't need to be told twice. As they made for the back door Jeff heard a sickening crunch and saw Dick Graham sprawling across the lazy susan full of salad. Jeff and Chappy got Mr McAlister down the steps and across the lawn to the boat. They lifted it for him to climb under and Jeff said: "Bob, you'll be fine here, don't worry. We'll come get you when this has quietened down."

Back in the house punches were flying in the balmy evening air. Mark Munro and Stanley the dog had taken their leave. Duke Boyd and Greg Tucker were hiding in a wardrobe. Salad splattered the walls and glass crunched underfoot.

The violence stopped as suddenly as it started, leaving everyone in shock, even the perpetrators. *Surfer* magazine's correspondent Drew Kampion arrived just a few minutes later.

"Outside is a pickup truck. Six or seven Hawaiians are in the open bed drinking Primo and singing very sad, very nostalgic Hawaiian songs. Other Hawaiians and a few haoles stand around, some joining in, tentatively. The night is very dark and the light from Hakman's kitchen daylights up one side of the pickup. All things seem as they should. Except Nat Young looks like he's seen a ghost (has he?) and the small group with which he stands is conspicuously silent."

(Kampion, incidentally, was the only one to report fully the events of the Good Karma Party, other correspondents evidently having been muzzled by the widely-held view that grown-ups like Bob McAlister would throw their money at professional tiddly-winks rather than give surfing a dime, if the world at large were to hear about the thugs, the drugs and the other normal North Shore stuff.)

Sheeeit! Bob McFuckingAlister!

At least two hours had passed. The boozy brethren inside were swaying to the sweet sound of the old songs, arm in arm. Clyde was sorry. Eddie was sorry. Butch was passed out somewhere. Dick Graham had broken ribs, but was putting a brave face on it. The problems of the world had been resolved. Butch was in the Expression Session. Shoot, Butch had always been in the Expression Session! Some prick just forgot to tell him.

Then Chappy looked at Jeff across the room. Oh, no! Oh, yes. The boat. The Bob.

"Bob, Bob, you okay there?"

"I'm fine. Can I come out now?"

After the Good Karma Party, the actual Golden Breed Expression Session was something of an anti-climax. The surfers, given the vote on when to stage it, outsmarted themselves and, with the waiting time running out, had to settle for a mediocre day at Rocky Point. And since it wasn't really a contest, none of the recreational surfers came out of the water to allow it to proceed. The casual observer would have had no idea what was going on, and the television crew had the same problem. Time had run out and the Smirnoff was set to begin, but with nowhere near enough footage in the can, the Expression Session made a dash to Maui, where it was concluded in good surf around Lahaina, but with a much diminished cast.

Windy Sunset, Jeff and Eddie Aikau on a west peak.

CHAPTER 17

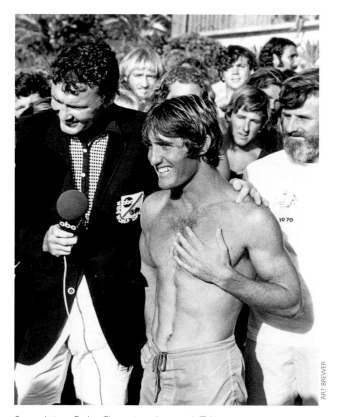

Second time Duke Champion chats with TV.

The fact that Jeff Hakman was invited to the sixth annual Duke Kahanamoku Invitational in December 1970 is testament to the fact that the times were changing. Unwanted in '69 and with criminal charges hanging over his head for much of the year since, the first Duke champion and former Duke team rider was considered an extremely unlikely starter.

Thirteen years younger than the Makaha International, the Duke meet did not have the same strong cultural slant, but its founder Kimo Wilder McVay, and his board of upstanding businessmen and citizens, nevertheless took great pride in their belief that the contest kept the spirit of the Duke alive. There were standards of conduct. It took two ministers of religion to get the thing started, for Christ's sake! One to do the invocation, one to read the benediction. And you didn't just come by a Duke invite. You had to earn it, in the surf and out.

To their eternal credit, the board of the Duke meet listened to their poll and not to their ingrained prejudices. Jeff was still charged with drug offences, but he was the stand-out surfer on the North Shore, a former champion and undoubtedly a future one. They put him in, and they must have breathed a huge sigh of relief when the charges against him were dropped several weeks before the event.

Jeff had told Dick Graham: "If they invite me I'm gonna win it". And he meant it. The night before the contest he couldn't sleep.

He recalls: "The surf was on the way up and I knew it was going to be good. The sets were shaking the house and the vibrations were coming up through my bed. I kept looking at my watch in the moonlight coming through the window, and wishing it would get light. In the end I just couldn't stand it, I was so amped up. I got up, put my board on the car and drove down to Sunset and sat on the beach in the dark, trying to pick out the conditions. I knew it was good, but I couldn't tell how good.

"As soon as there was a hint of grey on the horizon, I paddled out. I was in the lineup before it was light enough to pick it, and I took my first wave when it was still just the

predawn. It was twelve feet and I had it to myself for almost an hour. When other surfers started paddling out, I paddled in and sat on the beach again, waiting for the thing to start. I was loose, I was confident and I was totally focused."

In a generally indifferent winter for surf, the day of the Duke stood out like a beacon. As the preliminaries wore on, the trade winds picked up strength and caressed the faces of the ten to fifteen feet north-west peaks. The fierce spray made it difficult for some surfers, but Jeff sat high on his eight feet four inch Jim Turner mini-gun (a board he called Abba Zabba, because the plan shape was stretched like the candy of that name), knee-paddling for better vision and streaking into position ahead of the pack.

The final featured some of the heaviest names in surfing, all of them representative of the new performance direction in big wave riding. From Australia, Nat Young and Peter Drouyn; from the North Shore veteran power school, Paul Strauch and Barry Kanaiaupuni; Hawaiian stylists Billy Hamilton and Ryan Dotson; and from the new breed of '70s Hawaiian technique, Reno Abellira and Jeff Hakman.

Both Young and Drouyn started aggressively but midway through, Jeff saw the former world champion take off on a wave in front of another finalist. Nat looked likely to score an interference call, but Drouyn was on his heels, and the new card scoring system let both the spectators and the competitors know who was in the lead. With Young's interference still to be judged, the lead switched between the three.

Says Jeff: "It never occurred to me that I might not win. I was that focused. There were other guys out there surfing well – Reno, for example – but I knew it was going to be me, unless Drouyn did something spectacular."

With only a minute left on the clock, both Jeff and Drouyn were in the lineup and streaking towards an incoming set. There wasn't time to wait for the second, and Reno was paddling. A split second before his commitment to the twelve feet pitching barrel was complete, Reno thrust his legs into the water and pulled his weight back. He nodded to Jeff, who spun around and almost freefell, just held the line and carved a powerful turn off the face.

The siren sounded, the contest was Jeff's.

The thousand dollar purse was presented in a simple ceremony in front of the television cameras on the beach. Kimo McVay held out a calabash overflowing with dollar bills, which proved too much temptation for one young spectator, who snuck up from behind,

ART BREWER

Kimo McVay hands over $999 cash.

grabbed a dollar bill and ran. McVay generously made up the amount with a dollar out of his own pocket.

The resurrection of Jeff Hakman, professional surfer, was completed that winter, when he went on to take a third in the Makaha, behind Peter Drouyn and Felipe Pomar, and a first in the Hawaiian Professional Surfing Association's Haleiwa Open.

Professional, of course, was still a state of mind rather than a financial reality – Jeff's winnings for the entire season were less than he had made selling two pounds of dope the previous winter. But it suddenly seemed like it could happen, at least for the top echelon of the sport, and Jeff's performances in contests and in free surfing since December 1969 had placed him squarely in that elite club, along with Nat Young, Peter Drouyn, Barry Kanaiaupuni, David Nuuhiwa and Reno Abellira.

Jock Sutherland's military service had put him out of the picture somewhat, but asked who he regarded as the most impressive surfers in the world in an interview with *Surfer* magazine early in 1971, Jeff said: "If you could combine Barry, Jock and David, you'd just have the ultimate flash".

Part of Jeff's prize for winning the Duke was an all-expenses paid trip to Peru to compete in the Peruvian championships in February. There had long been a loose affiliation between Club Waikiki in Lima and Honolulu's Outrigger Canoe Club, and the head honcho of surfing in Peru, businessman Eduardo Arena, just happened to be a close friend of Hawaiian surfing supremo George Downing. The deal was that Downing would bring the top placegetters down for a week of surfing and partying, while lending a little international gloss to the event.

Jeff was amazed when he saw how surfing operated in Peru. In a throwback to the pre-missionary days in Hawaii when surfers really did rule, the surfers were at the top of the stack of Peruvian society. The sport was basically run by a small cartel of obscenely wealthy businessmen who kept summer homes on the cliffs outside the resort town of Punta Hermosa, with motor cruisers of Queen Mary proportions anchored in the bays below. Just a little way along the cliffs from the mansions was Punta Rocas, a surf spot famous for its large but mushy waves. Jeff managed to get a couple of surfs in here, but as soon as the Hawaiian contingent arrived, the green light had gone on for the parties to begin.

The master of the game at his best at Sunset, 1970.

The principal venue for the all night sessions of drinking, dancing and debauching was the Club Waikiki in the exclusive Mira Flores section of Lima. Here the young heroes of the surf scene disported themselves nightly, usually with a bevy of socialite beauties. On the surface it seemed that the deal was a snappy, cleancut bossa nova then bed, but just below the surface, the famous Peruvian hospitality opened up in new and different ways.

Jeff had tried cocaine on several occasions at parties in California and a couple of times on the North Shore. In Peru it was everywhere.

"At private parties guys would walk around with a pisco sour in one hand and a tube of coke in the other. They'd just pour it out on the backs of their hands and offer it to you. I remember standing in one place at a party one night, and when I looked down I'd dumped more on the floor than went up my nose. In fact there was more on the floor than I'd ever seen before.

"It was pure Peruvian flake and the standard deal with visiting surfers was one ounce for one good board. I thought it was a pretty neat drug at the time – kept you up all night so you could party more – and I might have traded my board, except that I knew a surfer there who was doing a roaring trade smuggling coke in hollowed out boards, and he gave me a couple of ounces to play around with."

It didn't take Jeff long to experience the downside of the drug. He went home to Eduardo Arena's guest villa in the early hours of the morning after a particularly heavy session, and lay on the bed with his heart palpitating. He was wide awake, totally wired and scared.

"I'd never experienced anything like it. I thought for sure I was going to have a heart attack and die, and I considered waking up Eduardo and telling him what I'd done. But I couldn't, so I lay there and rode it out."

Between the hectic round of social engagements, the Peruvians found time to hold the contest, which Jeff won, with Peter Drouyn second again. Then it was back to Club Waikiki for a serious celebration.

At some point in the proceedings, someone got up on stage and announced that the winner and the runner up "had to fight the bull". Jeff recalls: "I'm thinking what bull? Then suddenly we're in fast cars, speeding out into the country to some bull fight. I was pretty fucked up by this time, but as we got closer I realised that this was a real bull fight we were going to. I mean, they couldn't be serious, could they? There were some bottles of wine being passed around in the car, so I grabbed one and took a few slugs just in case."

When they arrived at the bull ring the Peruvians explained that tradition required Jeff to fight the bull first. "But don't worry, Jeff. It's only a baby bull and its horns have been chopped off."

They sat in the stands and watched two bull fights. Serious bull fights with a couple of thousand people going wild as the matadors flirted with death. Jeff felt sick. He drank more wine. The matador killed the bull and a tractor appeared and carted the carcass away.

Jeff: "They are insisting that now it's my turn. I'm pretty greased up by now, so I get in the friggin' bull ring and everyone starts cheering wildly, and in comes this big bull. Not a baby bull, not a bull with its horns chopped off. A big, big bull. About three feet between its horns, so that when it swings its head, it's got a span of about ten feet. And I've got a cape that's about three feet.

"When the bull focused on me I could feel my heart trying to leap out of my chest. Waimea Bay or big Sunset had nothing on this. I was just terrified. The bull started coming and I tried to hold my ground as long as possible...then I dropped the cape and ran."

The crowd went beserk as Jeff scrambled behind a barricade, then suddenly the Peruvians and Drouyn were in the ring too, the arena swamped with cheering and singing, and, of course, drinking.

It was party time again.

CHAPTER 18

During 1970 Jeff had been one of the surfers featured in "Cosmic Children", a movie made by Hal Jepsen. Jeff liked the quiet, easy-going Jepsen, a Californian whose other interests included stamp collecting and corresponding with pen pals, so when Jepsen invited him to travel to Europe in the late summer of '71 to help promote Cosmic Children and do some filming for its sequel, Jeff was happy to accept.

When he had finished his surf school season in Waikiki (with Felipe Pomar now that Paul Strauch had retired) Jeff joined Jepsen in Los Angeles where they caught a Lufthansa charter flight to Frankfurt.

Europe was pretty much unknown surf territory in those days, but even Jeff knew there was no surf in Frankfurt. "I want to meet my pen pal and trade some stamps," Jepsen explained. Jeff had a momentary flashback to his trip to Nebraska to meet Curt Mastalka's grandmother, but in fact the time in Frankfurt was enjoyable and productive. They bought an old Volkswagen bug, loaded up the boards and cameras and took off towards the Atlantic coast of France.

Says Jeff: "We didn't really know where we were going, except to Biarritz of course, but the idea was to try and find some surf along the way, and we didn't have a clue. There was nothing like the autoroute system of today. We just seemed to be cruising along these little country roads for days. And then we hit the coast road heading south and I saw a sign to Hossegor. I remembered the name, seeing pictures of Mark Martinson and Keith Paull surfing there, so I told Hal to turn in.

"We drove in towards the beach and followed the road down to just north of the village. It was five in the afternoon, the surf was glassy, six to eight feet, just beautiful and one guy out in the water. Surfing naked.

"I watched him for a bit, taking off and leaning into these big bottom turns with his dick hanging out, and I suddenly flashed it's my friend Mike Miller from Hawaii. So I paddled out and said hi. Michael said hi and we kept surfing together. I never asked him why

Biarritz, 1971. Jeff and Hal Jepsen meet the local crew.

he was naked and he didn't mention it. It seemed like the most natural thing in the world."

Miller, a long-time North Shore big wave rider and all-round waterman, helped Jeff and Jepsen rent a little country house nearby, and for the next several weeks they based themselves at the consistently good beach breaks of Hossegor while making forays into the French surf centre of Biarritz to promote the movie.

Says Jeff: "It wasn't like it is today in France. The whole summer scene just shut down at the end of August, and this was September. There weren't many shops or cafes still open, and almost no one around. There was certainly no nightlife, but there was good surf every day. And then suddenly, from out of nowhere, everyone came. Gerry Lopez arrived with Brian Seurrat, Brad McCaul on his way back from South Africa and Morocco, Mike Tabeling from the East Coast, Mike Diffenderfer showed up...It was like Honolua Bay in '67 all over again. There just seemed to be this magnetic force at work."

That first trip to France instilled in Jeff a love of the French way of life, the countryside, the food, the smells, the people, the joie de vivre, and, of course, the surf. He promised himself he would return.

When Jeff returned to Hawaii in mid-October he discovered he had topped the Duke poll, being voted number one invitee for the meet by a selection panel of surfers and officials. Although this was by no means a definitive rating (in fact in the past it had been one of the most trenchantly criticised ratings systems in the sport), in 1971 the Duke was wearing a new look under contest director Chuck Shipman, and its invitee list had a new credibility.

"Hakman voted No 1 Surfer" trumpeted the same Honolulu newspapers which had earlier reported his drug charge arrest. And if few people really believed that topping the Duke poll made you the best surfer in the world, fewer still would have denied that Jeff Hakman deserved the accolade that year as much as anyone.

Behind Jeff on the poll came Barry Kanaiaupuni, Reno Abellira, Nat Young, Gerry Lopez and Joey Cabell. Cabell was beginning to fade, more interested in skiing and his restaurant business, Young, the 1970 Smirnoff champion, was pursuing a country soul lifestyle, and the others were where it was at in Hawaiian surfing. The Brewer twins, Lopez and Abellira, were graceful pilots of radical, speedline equipment, Kanaiaupuni was power personified and technically, one of the masters of Sunset, and Jeff...well, Jeff was unique.

Steve Pezman had recently been installed as *Surfer* magazine's editor and publisher, and he kept a close watch on the masters of the game. In 1996 he recalled: "Hakman was the original surfer chimp, short legs, long arms, very strong...He'd just plant those feet of his in a wide stance, low centre of gravity, and just fly all over the place. Perfect control in the most radical situations. There was no one doing what he was doing."

You had to look quite a way further down the poll to see what Shipman and his selection panel were doing to revitalise the Duke, because there you found the next generation, names like Sam Hawk and Terry Fitzgerald. Californian and Australian respectively, they had arrived the previous winter and both had fallen under the Brewer spell. Hawk, from Huntington Beach, hung out with Gary Chapman and his brother Owl. Fitzgerald, from Narrabeen in Sydney, hung out with his wife.

In a 1990 *Surfer* interview, Dick Brewer recalled seeing Fitzgerald for the first time at Rocky Point in 1970: "He was different and he had to prove himself, but I recognised him as the best surfer in the world – the best I'd ever seen in fact – because of his speed lines...I invited him to stay on Kauai with me for a couple of weeks, and that turned into six months".

The Brewer-influenced Terry Fitzgerald started to turn heads on the North Shore. Says Jeff: "After he hooked up with Brewer he just exploded onto the scene. He was loud, colourful and flamboyant. His whole act was like blam! But he surfed beautifully, just beautifully."

Jeff was invited to the season opener, the Smirnoff Pro, and finished third behind Billy Hamilton and surprise winner, South African Gavin Rudolph. Then came the Duke.

The contest was called with Sunset Beach holding a solid ten to fifteen feet swell fanned by a strong offshore breeze. By the time the first heat was in the water, however, the wind

The "original surf chimp", legs, knees and butt in power drive.

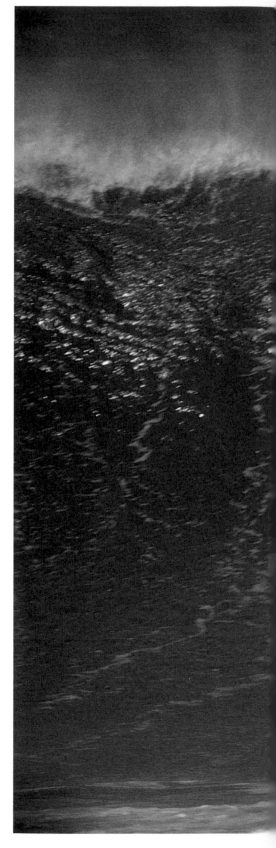

Above: *Yokahama Bay, 1971.*

Right: *Surf chimp again. Low centre of gravity, maximum turning power.*

his third in seven years

Jeff wins another Duke

By KEN KOBAYASHI
Advertiser Sports Writer

Jeff Hakman doesn't own that Duke Kahanamoku Surfing Classic. It only looks that way. Really.

The little 5-7, 140 pound surfer complicated the matter yesterday by winning $1,000 and his third Duke title in the meet's seven year history.

THAT'S LIKE Jack Nicklaus taking home three of the last seven U.S. Opens.

It's unprecedented.

No surfer has ever dominated any meet of the Duke's calibre the way Hakman has, winning in 1965—the first year of the meet, last year, and now yesterday in perhaps the most trying contest of them all.

Winds up to 35 m.p.h. knocked down wires and a utility pole at Sunset Beach, the Duke's site for the seventh straight time, and made the eight to 14-foot waves even harder to calculate and ride than usual.

"IT'S LIKE a hurricane, Chuck Shipman, executive director of the meet summed up correctly. "Wind, rain, everything."

The conditions obviously bothered the 24 surfers going after the $2,625 up for grabs. There were more spills than usual during the five hours-plus of competition. In the first 25 minutes of the final alone, four of the eight riders lost their boards, and later, even Hakman himself had to take the long swim to shore.

But the 23-year-old champ left nothing in doubt from the start of the one-hour, 15-minute final that it was to be his day at Sunset.

He quickly caught three waves for good scores, took a spill on the fourth, and then got a brilliant fifth ride to take the early lead.

EVERYONE KNEW Hakman was hot by then, and he got hotter. He kept his lead and then cinched the title with 20 minutes left with a tube-ride on a 12-foot wave for the best ride of the long day.

Hakman, son of tennis star Doris Hakman, rode a dozen waves in all, most in the final. That was good for firsts from all five judges.

Billy Hamilton was runner-up for the second time in a row. He was No. 2 at the Smirnoff two weeks ago. He made a fine comeback in the final after starting out at fifth and sixth.

Eddie Aikau, as if it were the Smirnoff all over again, had to go against his brother Clyde. Eddie ended up third and Clyde fifth.

California's Corky Carroll, the only goofy-footer among the finalists, finished fourth. Australia's only entry, Terry Fitzgerald, came in sixth. Duke's 1968 champ Mike Doyle from California was seventh. And Ben Aipa just didn't get enough rides to take eighth.

AS STRONG as the wind was, the gusts weren't the only adverse conditions. A strong rip carried boards in toward shore and then out to sea, as Fitzgerald and Jimmy Jones know.

In their semi-final heat, both were wiped out and then had to chase their boards for aboua a half-mile. It took them about 25 minutes during that 50-minute semi-final and for Jones, it was disastrous. Before his spill, he had the lead. When he came back, he found himself in sixth place—out of the money, and only about five minutes left to go.

To make it worse, his board was actually taken out to sea by a surfer who used it to chase Fitzgerald's board.

FINAL

1. Jeff Hakman (Hawaii) $1,000; 2. Billy Hamilton (Hawaii) $500; 3. Eddie Aikau (Hawaii) $300; 4. Corky Carroll (Calif.) $250; 5. Clyde Aikau (Hawaii) $200; 6. Terry Fitzgerald (Australia) $150; 7. Mike Doyle (Calif.) $150; 8. Ben Aipa (Hawaii) $100.

SEMI-FINAL

1. Fitzgerald (Aust.), 2. Carroll (Cal-

and today, the Masters

Big time surfing continues today with the Hawaii Masters event on the Banzai Pipeline.

Top prize of $500 is at stake with six top surfers competing, headed by Jeff Hakman, who yesterday won his third Duke Kahanamoku crown.

Also in the event, which starts at 9 a.m., are Corky Carroll, Gerry Lopez, Jock Sutherland, Butch Van Artsdalen and Jim Blears.

The ABC network will televise the two-hour program.

had strengthened to near gale force. Experience told the tale in the elimination heats, with Sunset veterans like Billy Hamilton and Clyde and Eddie Aikau breezing through on clever wave selection. Jeff rode an eight feet seven inch Golden Breed, plenty of flotation but fine lines, once again giving him better vision in the adverse conditions, and went straight into the final looking every inch a winner.

The expected challenge from Terry Fitzgerald almost evaporated when the Australian lost his board and the wind took hold of it and blew it out to sea. But he somehow managed to retrieve it in time and went on to win the semi-final. Says Fitzgerald: "I had to swim outside Kammieland to get the board and it took most of my energy. I only had two waves to that point, but I managed to get into the lineup for one more before the hooter went. Fortunately it was a good one and I won the semi."

The final was classic Hakman. He hit early and he hit hard, catching three high scoring rides before the others had two. Even when he uncharacteristically caught a rail and had to swim to the beach, Jeff's victory was never in doubt. His third Duke title in seven years was his easiest.

Says Fitzgerald: "Jeff won it by surfing on his own terms. He was ahead of yesterday and he knew he didn't need to be as radical as tomorrow. It was just intelligent contest surfing."

But the North Shore contest season wasn't quite over. A week after the Duke, the Pipeline Masters made its debut. Essentially a made-for-TV deal, the idea was to throw the best six Pipeline surfers into the lineup when it was perfect and let them jam for an hour while the cameras whirred. Once again, conditions conspired to defeat a good idea. With waiting time running out, the contest was called in six to eight feet windblown surf.

One by one the competitors arrived, Jeff, Jock Sutherland, Jimmy Blears, Billy Hamilton, Corky Carroll and, of course, Gerry...No Lopez. The organisers panicked. How could you have a Pipeline Masters without the reigning Mr Pipeline? But Gerry was a no-show and Mike Armstrong snuck in as first alternate.

Jeff recalls: "It felt kind of weird surfing this thing without Gerry, and it was real low-key. Just the cameras and Lord Tallyho Blears sitting at a card table with a microphone. Anyway, we paddled out there and the swell just wasn't quite right, difficult conditions. It boiled down to wave selection, and I was very strong in that area, but I was still surprised that I won. Backsiders just didn't handle Pipe that well back then.

"I really don't think I would have beaten Gerry. We found out later that he'd run into Corky Carroll an hour or so before the event, and Corky had apparently told him it wasn't on. Corky always did play hard."

Far left: Just like Jack Nicklaus, says the Honolulu Advertiser.

Opposite and below: *Classic Maalaea sequence, 1972*

SEQUENCE STEVE WILKINGS

103

On the tour, Peru, 1972.

Being both defending champion and the Duke winner again, Jeff should have had two tickets to Peru in February 1972. He settled for one. This time there was a bigger Hawaiian contingent, including Gerry Lopez, George Downing's son Keone and the newest star to emerge from the ruck at Ala Moana, Afro-haired Larry Bertleman.

Jeff recalls: "It was a similar deal to the year before – a little bit of surfing, parties, booze, coke, people running rampant and getting fucked up. Hey, it was great! I'm not sure how old Larry was, but very young, and one night he had so *much* fun he fell into a plate glass window at a party and almost went straight through it. Gerry and I realised he was bad news and we kinda picked him up off the floor, and this other guest offers his beach house for Larry to rest up. So we drag Larry around to this adobe beach house, and up the stairs to the loft bedroom and lay him down. This was a pretty neat bedroom, by the way. Very 1972. About a dozen mobiles hanging from the roof, and tapestries on the walls. We put Larry down and head back to the party.

"A couple of hours later we go back there to pick him up, or maybe to do more coke, I forget, and the second we walk through the door we know we got trouble. The place is a mess. We follow a trail of wreckage up the stairs to the bedroom and Larry's not there. In his place is this little duck. This real duck! The room is just demolished. We race outside and there's a trail of debris out the back door and through the yard, and footprints of dirt. But Larry's gone, and we've lost the trail."

The next morning Jeff was woken by a call from team manager George Downing. "Did you guys see Larry last night?"

"Larry? Oh, ah, yeah, maybe."

"Was he okay?"

"Yeah, sure. Why?"

"Because I got a big problem with the Punta Hermosa police. They say Larry's the monster who was roaming the streets last night and raiding people's kitchens. I know that can't be right, so I'm gonna get Eduardo and Hector Vallarde and go talk to them."

Jeff recalled Hector Vallarde's performance in evading the law after his beach driving at San Diego in 1966, and figured Larry would be okay. But the legend of the Monster of Punta Hermosa, who crawled around in the dirt on all fours and stole food from decent people's kitchens, was only just beginning.

And Larry Bertleman would have to live with it throughout his illustrious professional surfing career.

Last wave of the day, Outside Pipeline, 1972.

CHAPTER 19

Jeff with Billy Hamilton at Jeffrey's Bay, 1972.

The top three placegetters in the 1971 Smirnoff Pro won round-trip tickets to South Africa to compete in that country's only professional surfing event, the Gunston, plus a thirty day African surf safari compliments of the South African Surfing Association. However, because South Africa's own Gavin Rudolph had won the Smirnoff, the invitation was extended to second, third and fourth, Billy Hamilton, Jeff and Eddie Aikau.

Eddie Aikau couldn't make the safari, so Jeff and Bill Hamilton flew down to Johannesburg, where they met up with representatives of the Gunston cigarette company and their co-sponsor, Seven Seas Liquor, and flew on to Cape Town to start their grand tour.

At that time worldwide opposition to South Africa's apartheid system had reached such proportions that there were riots whenever a South African sporting team (like the rugby union Springboks) toured another country. The anti-apartheid movement, led by a young Englishman named Peter Hain, sought nothing less than complete sporting and cultural isolation of the Republic until it abandoned its racist policies towards the black majority of its citizens.

The movement had become so strong globally that it even permeated Hawaii's North Shore. At Punahou School, Jeff had greatly respected a fellow student named Lee Wy Diu, a polio victim who could barely walk, but who surfed Pipeline on his hands and knees on a conventional surfboard. Lee had gone on to become a lawyer and political activist in Honolulu, and when he heard about Jeff's forthcoming trip to South Africa, he approached him at Rocky Point one day.

"You can't go, Jeff. You must not go, you'll be playing right into their hands."

Jeff wanted to go. He'd wanted to go since he saw Hynson and August surfing "Bruce's Beauties" in the 1964 Bruce Brown movie The Endless Summer. Sure, he'd heard about apartheid, but that was politics and he was a sportsman. And how can you knock a place if you haven't been there? These were the standard rationales of the time, and they were enough for Jeff.

At Cape Town the visiting surfers were bundled into two big Fords with Gunston and Seven Seas signwriting all over them and the safari began. At various points along the way they were joined by South Africa's leading surfers, Gavin Rudolph, Peers Pittard, Jonathon Parmaan and a little kid named Shaun Tomson who surfed up a storm on a tiny fish board. They surfed near-perfect Jeffrey's Bay, partied all night with the girls of Port Elizabeth (where they had to take part in an official street parade), saw elephants and giraffes in the wild at a game reserve, stayed at exclusive little country hotels and generally had a ball.

The South African surfers had plenty of "Durban Poison", a particularly effective strain of dope, and Hamilton and Jeff passed long and pleasant hours in the back of the chauffeured Ford, stoned to the gills. At a piss stop in the middle of the Transkei, they were suddenly surrounded by black men and boys with white paint all over their faces. The Africaans driver, who by this stage was thoroughly disgusted with his dopier passengers, explained: "Puberty rites." He sat in the driver's seat staring straight ahead while Jeff and Billy clowned around with their new friends.

Jeff suddenly remembered the bootie in the trunk. "Hey, you guys smoke?" He mimicked the drawback and they all nodded extravagantly and giggled. The Gunston people had thoughtfully provided about a hundred cartons of their filter-tipped product, so Jeff and Billy opened the trunk and started throwing cigarette packs into the crowd. There was a near-riot.

When they finally arrived in Durban for the contest, they were taken to oceanfront rooms at the ritzy Malibu Hotel, overlooking the Bay of Plenty and the city's major surf spots and whites only beaches. Then Eddie arrived.

The people at the helm of South African surfing were amongst the most respected businessmen in Durban, savvy operators like Peter Burness and Shaun Tomson's father Ernie. But when it came to understanding their own government's racist policies, they appear to have had a rather large blind spot. Did it not occur to any of them that Eddie Aikau, the nearest thing to a pure-blood Hawaiian you could find in the second half of the twentieth century, was not exactly a blue-eyed blond? When Aikau arrived in the lobby of the Malibu Hotel to check in, he was told politely but firmly that he was the wrong colour. Eddie was not happy. Not only was he the wrong colour for any of Durban's upmarket hotels, he was the wrong colour for the beach at which he was expected to compete!

There was instant panic and total embarrassment. Hurried negotiations with government authorities resulted in special beach privileges being granted for the duration of the meet, but the Malibu Hotel wasn't having any of this bolshie bleeding heart liberal bullshit. Let one in and they'll take over, exsair. Ernie Tomson found a face-saving solution by putting Eddie up at his own beachfront apartment a few doors along from the hotel, and the SASA officials went out of their way to keep Eddie entertained twenty-four hours a day.

But the damage had been done. Eddie was an Aikau, for Christ's sake! In Hawaii the Aikaus were almost like royalty! Eddie kept his own counsel but he nursed a deep and bitter hurt. The Durban press got hold of the story and raised the question: would this treatment of Aikau lead to a boycott of the Gunston by the Hawaiian team? On that score the organisers need not have worried. Both Jeff and Billy Hamilton took the view that if blacks weren't allowed in the hotel, it was stupid but that was the way things were here. Besides, Eddie hadn't even talked to them about the issue, and seemed to be over it.

This naive assumption was perhaps also coloured a little by the fact that at that time neither Hamilton nor Jeff were particularly close to the Aikaus. Just eighteen months earlier Eddie and Clyde had been part of the mob that tore Jeff's place apart and beat up on Dick Graham, and while that episode had been forgiven and forgotten, Jeff and Eddie did not have regular heart to hearts.

Says Jeff: "Maybe we were being selfish, maybe we just didn't think the whole thing through, but if Eddie had been camped in some slum while we were at the Malibu Hotel, I'm sure we would have seen it differently. But Eddie was living in more luxury than we were, and he never said a thing to us."

The A-frame at Pupukea.

Jeff got local Australian-born shaper Darryl Holmes to build him two boards to suit the Durban beach breaks (which could vary from small to quite large and powerful) and went into heavy training in the leadup to the contest. He was loose and confident when the meet began in small Bay of Plenty lefts, and progressed easily to the final. Then overnight the swell jumped, and the finalists jumped off the groyne into crunching eight to ten feet sets.

The surf was ideally suited to Jeff's power-gliding style, and he quickly racked up three high-scoring rides while the others, Shaun Tomson, Gavin Rudolph, Peers Pittard, Jonathon Parmaan and Mike Esposito, had only one apiece. After another good ride, he found himself caught inside with Esposito and Parmaan. A ten feet wave broke right on their heads, and while Jeff popped up okay, the other two surfers lost their boards and had to swim to the beach. Jeff started paddling again and realised that three more waves were going to break on him. He looked at his watch. Fifteen minutes to go. Shit, no one was gonna catch him. He turned around and caught a broken wave to the beach.

When the final siren went, Jeff Hakman, the world's best contest surfer, was sitting in the competitors' tent with his feet up and his second beer at his lips. It was perhaps the only time in his surfing career that arrogance ever crept into Jeff's act. But it could be argued that he could afford to be arrogant. He won easily.

The final chapter of the month-long South African soiree had all the elements of farce. In previous years, the Gunston had been won by foreigners – Midget Farrelly in 1970, Brad McCaul in '71 – who had left South Africa with the money, apparently in contravention of another stupid law, so in 1972 alien competitors had been made to sign a declaration that they would not accept any prize money. At the presentation ceremony in front of a huge Durban crowd, the managing director of Gunston Tobacco handed Jeff a cheque for two thousand rand, which he was allowed to hold for all of ten minutes while the appropriate photographs were taken.

Back in Hawaii Eddie Aikau told a reporter from the *Honolulu Advertiser* about the humiliating experience of not being allowed to stay in the same hotel as Jeff and Billy. He was quoted as saying, "My Hawaiian team mates abandoned me".

Billy Hamilton saw it from a slightly different perspective. In his account of the trip, published in *Surfer* magazine (something of a public relations coup for the South African government), he wrote: "An interesting sidelight of the event was brought about by the attendance of Eddie Aikau, who, with his dark brown Hawaiian tan and characteristic Island features, was the target of a few tossed glances from the predominantly white gathering".

Interesting sidelight?

Hamilton also wrote: "Generally, the situation among the dark-skinned people is accepted; they are content with their working positions and the roles they play in the structure of society along with their European counterparts". Or so it no doubt seemed from the smoky back seat of the Ford.

That summer Jeff became a landowner. He and another transplanted Californian surfer, Bill Sickler, bought an acre lot in the recently-opened up Pupukea Highlands estate above Waimea Bay. They put twelve thousand dollars down, bought the land for twenty four thousand and put another twenty four thousand into the construction of a simple A-frame cottage. It was a wise investment since North Shore rentals were becoming harder to get and ridiculously over-priced. And Jeff surprised himself by being exceedingly house-proud.

In September San Diego played host to the world titles again, but much had changed in the six years since Nat Young had emerged triumphant at Ocean Beach. The professional scene had stolen most of the thunder, and the last truly representative world amateur surfing championships were relatively low key.

Hawaii's Jimmy Blears won in trashy three feet waves, but most of the real action took place away from the beach.

Says Jeff: "I hadn't been to a world contest since 1966, when it was all girls and psychedelics. In '72 it was all girls and cocaine. It was a fuckin' snowstorm. I remember driving

around in San Diego with some Peruvians one night, snorting coke from a bag as we went along. Eventually we ran out, so the guy driving, who was no more than eighteen, pulled up, went to the trunk and brought back a huge pound bag and just opened it up. I couldn't believe my eyes."

It was also the year of the new wave of Australians. Afro-haired Terry Fitzgerald was just twenty-two, but he was the veteran in a team that included Paul Neilsen, Peter Townend, Ian Cairns, Mark Warren, Wayne "Rabbit" Bartholomew, Grant "Dappa" Oliver and a brooding, manic Queenslander named Michael Peterson. Apart from Fitzgerald, Jeff had never seen nor heard of any of them, but they were the wild men at every party and they were all over the junky waves with near-vertical, staccato moves on their wide little boards. Townend, who finished third in the contest, was the only one who surfed with any semblance of California style. The rest of them had a unique, energetic approach that was almost exhausting to watch.

Jeff recalls: "It seemed like every year a hot new Aussie would pop up and become a threat. Like one year it'd be Keith Paull, the next year Drouyn, the next year Fitz. Then suddenly in San Diego there's a dozen of them, and they're all red hot! I thought, Jesus, I better watch out."

Above: *Jeff and friends at the Pupukea house.*
Above left: *Mark Warren…"unique energetic approach".*

CHAPTER 20

Off The Wall, 1972.

While most of the Australians headed straight home after the 1972 world titles in San Diego, Paul Neilsen and his older brother Ricky got off the plane in Hawaii and set up house on the North Shore at Sunset Point. It was unheard of for a touring contest pro to arrive on the North Shore this early in the season and gave some of the long-time locals heartburn when they considered what might happen if all the pros came in October and stayed until February.

But they didn't have to worry about the brothers Neilsen. They were fun-loving, happy-go-lucky types who observed the pecking order etiquette in the water and loved to drink beer and talk story almost as much as the Hawaiians. (In fact they were all but adopted by the Aikau clan, who saw them as soul brothers.) Brought up in the spinning, spitting sand bottom barrels of Burleigh Heads and Kirra on Queensland's Gold Coast, they were deep tube riders with an angular approach that continually put them into the most critical part of the wave. Ricky was a very good surfer, but Paul was exceptional. Just twenty years old, he was lean, muscular and very strong. He was a fast paddler with excellent wave judgment; he was fearless in big waves and he did his stuff with an absolute economy of action. In short, he was Jeff Hakman.

The Neilsens were shameless party boys who loved to hit the night clubs of Waikiki in their best aloha shirts and puka shell necklaces, but they also had rigid and well known views about the infiltration of the dope culture into surfing. (At the Australian team hotel in San Diego, the team managers had to break up a brawl after Ricky had discovered another surfer's dope stash and flushed it down the toilet.) If the Neilsens had known about Jeff's adventures in Baja and Beirut things might have been different; as it was, they didn't and they became the firmest of friends.

Says Jeff: "I liked them a lot. Everyone did. They had this raw energy and such a sense of fun. And by the time the contests were due to start, Paul had been surfing Sunset nearly every day for a month and he was red hot, just totally tuned. He was a good surfer for a

Sunset lineup. A sight for sore eyes.

Smirnoff, 1972 at Haleiwa. Nice wave, but not enough.

lot of years – he's still a good surfer – but he would never surf better than he did on the North Shore that fall."

The 1972 Smirnoff boasted the biggest purse of any contest in professional surfing's short history, with five thousand dollars for first place. And when a huge swell hit two days before the start of the waiting period, it seemed it would be won in appropriately challenging conditions. But on the morning of November 20, Sunset was reeling under twenty feet sets and contest director Fred Hemmings called the meet on and moved it to Haleiwa, where the swell was manageable, if difficult at eight to ten feet. The North Shore veterans were counselling him to wait another day until Sunset had straightened out, but Hemmings had the sponsors and the camera crews to think about, and he saw contestable waves right now.

Paul Neilsen surfed brilliantly throughout the preliminaries, and he and Grant Oliver were the two Australians to advance to the final, along with Eddie Aikau, Sam Hawk, Gerry Lopez and Jeff. (In fact, "Dappa" Oliver had been suffering from a stomach virus and spent most of the day running to the toilets. By the time he reached the final, he was totally drained.)

Perhaps realising that he didn't have the energy to go the distance in the forty-five minute final, Dappa went at it like a freight train from the moment the siren signalled the

Pulling out all the stops, '72 Smirnoff.

start. Neilsen matched him move for move, both of them all over the face on the medium-sized waves while the Hawaiians waited outside for the bigger sets.

Says Jeff: "Dappa was just brilliant for about the first fifteen minutes. It was just a full-on assault, and Paul was in there with him. But then Dappa ran out of gas – you could really tell he was hurting – and Paul didn't. I started to get some good outside waves and I felt I was making ground on him. By the last fifteen minutes it was down to me and Paul and he was all over me, paddling around me, hassling for all he was worth. No matter how close we'd become, he was a tough sonofabitch in competition. It was real, real close, and then he took off on a good one right next to me and moments later I could hear them hooting on the beach and I knew I was in trouble."

Neilsen took out the biggest purse in surfing with Jeff second and Dappa Oliver third. This brought on a celebration that was still unfolding two days later when Jeff called into Kammie's Food Mart at Sunset Beach for some groceries and ran into Clyde Aikau.

"Hey, Jeff bra, we havin' a little party at Neilsen's place. Big fun, huh! Pop be there (Pop Aikau, the patriarch of the clan), we got some swipe, you come, huh!"

Jeff was expecting his new girlfriend, Cecilia, to arrive at any moment and he had in

113

Congratulations, Jeff.

mind a fairly quiet and romantic evening, besides he'd already done two nights of celebrating with Neilsen and the thrill was wearing off. "Well, thanks, Clyde. I'll sure try."

"You come, Jeff, you come, huh?"

Jeff and Cecilia were in bed at the Pupukea A-frame around ten that evening when the front door was suddenly kicked open and the Aikau brothers and a few of their friends stood in a semi-circle around the foot of the bed. Clyde did the talking.

"Put some clothes on, Jeff. You come to the party."

"Oh, sure, Clyde. As a matter of fact we were just on our way."

They dressed and went to the party with their escort. "It was a good party," Jeff recalls.

Paul Neilsen continued his charge that busy five-meet winter with an incredible series of impossibly late take-offs at Sunset in the Duke Invitational, however he was called on a controversial interference ruling and missed out on a place while Jeff got a respectable third. But there was no doubt in anyone's mind that Neilsen had Jeff's mantle as best contest surfer in the world clearly in his sights.

The showdown between the two friends was set for the inaugural Hang Ten American Pro, the first contest to employ a new and revolutionary judging system devised by George Downing. Since money had come into the equation, the central argument against the standard twenty point judging system, which had been used since the birth of the Makaha International, was that it was too subjective. Contest directors tried to use a judging panel spread across the spectrum of age, cultural and geographic differences, but often it still all came down to one person's interpretation of what constituted "good surfing".

Downing's system was the first attempt to judge surfing as a series of skills with a known points value. As it said on the cover of the Hang Ten American Pro Championship Rule Book, "The rules...reflect an attempt to formulate a totally objective professional surfing scoring system in that a contestant will not be judged on style or exhibition of grace". This was considered unfortunate by a vast number of people who believed that style and grace were the essence of good surfing, but the Downing system was an honest and worthy attempt to make professional surfing contests fairer for all. It would take at least half a dozen years and many excruciatingly silly permutations (does anyone now recall Peter Drouyn's "effective cheating" rule at the first Stubbies meet?) before an objective system actually worked the way it was meant to, but Downing's Hang Ten system in 1972 was the grandfather of modern judging methodology.

Jeff sat in the Outrigger Canoe Club at Waikiki and listened intently as Downing went through the rule book, clause by clause. Contestants were to be scored on each manoeuvre executed over three rounds of surfing, with the highest cumulative score deciding the winner. The degree of difficulty was determined by wave size, with a bottom turn, for example, being worth ten points on a small wave (up to seven feet) but twenty points on a large wave (thirteen feet to eighteen feet). One of the manoeuvres listed was a new one on Jeff – the zigzag. This was nothing more than a directional change on the wave face, something you might do out of boredom while waiting for the next section to form, but it was worth points, and Jeff made a mental note of it.

The Hang Ten was held over two days in medium-sized Sunset waves, but by the end of the first day no one was in any doubt about who would take the four thousand dollar first place. Jeff Hakman had simply blitzed the new system, taking more waves and performing more manoeuvres than anyone else. No one was suggesting that Jeff was actually surfing better, but he was playing the game with ruthless efficiency. *Surfer* magazine correspondent Drew Kampion noted that Jeff won his first round heat with more than seven hundred points, while Terry Fitzgerald had only three hundred and fifty to win his.

Jeff recalls: "I was just able to adapt. I'd had more water time at Sunset than just about anyone else in the contest, and I knew the waves so well I could concentrate on the winning formula. The system was simple – it was just like this big adding machine, and the more waves you got and the more things you did, the more points you racked up. But the downside was obvious almost immediately. There was no allowance for finesse. I watched Gerry Lopez and Michael Peterson surfing in one heat. Gerry took the first set wave and surfed it smoothly and conservatively, carving lots of turns and cutbacks. Then Peterson took off in back of him on the next wave, way deep, just a beautiful wave. It was super critical and all he could do was hold his line and get completely tubed. It was the perfect Sunset tube, and he scored half as many points as Gerry."

This was the first and last time that the objective system beat Peterson, who went on to become its absolute master.

As for the much-touted showdown between Jeff and Paul Neilsen, it didn't eventuate. Neilsen's best season as a pro surfer had peaked just a little early. He surfed strongly for fourth (Barry Kanaiaupuni powered into second, with consistently smooth Peter Townend third) but he never looked like being a threat to Jeff. He told Drew Kampion: "Some surfers have an edge. Jeff Hakman has a consistency edge."

In fact, for Paul Neilsen the moment had passed, and while he remained a highly respected competitor around the world, he never again came so close to the summit of achievement.

The Hang Ten victory underscored what people in the know had been saying for more than a year, that in lieu of an official ratings, Jeff Hakman was the unofficial but undeniable world champion of professional surfing. He usually won, he was never out of the placings and, in the North Shore winter season alone, he took out seven thousand five hundred dollars of the twenty thousand total prize pool.

Drew Kampion summed up the Hakman enigma thus: "Be it the standard competitive format...or be it this new...type of event, Hakman is more consistently there, in contention and winning the money than anyone else. He puts aside emotion for comprehension, and deals very strictly with the realities of a situation...If professionalism is going to make it in surfing, as it more and more appears is the case, then it will be surfers like Jeff Hakman who will dominate the sport."

STEVE WILKINGS

Above: Television interview, 1972.
Below: Sunset, December 1972.

STEVE WILKINGS

CHAPTER 21

Paul Neilsen cranks a cutback at Bells Beach.

In 1973 the long-running Bells Beach Easter Classic in Australia's cold southern waters went professional, signalling the much-anticipated emergence of a world professional surfing tour. A one-meet tour was not enough to entice Jeff nor many of the other Hawaiians to make the long journey "down under", but Gerry Lopez had been passing through, doing some promotional work for the Australian Golden Breed franchise, and came back with glowing reports of the inaugural pro Bells, held in the solid autumnal swells of Victoria's west coast.

Throughout the North Shore winter of '73 the Australians were full of talk of a two-meet tour for real money in 1974. As well as the Bells meet, sponsored by Rip Curl Wetsuits, the Coca Cola corporation and a Sydney radio station were said to be putting up a huge purse to make their new event the most lucrative in the world. Jeff's 1973 North Shore form (third in the Duke, second in the Smirnoff and fourth in the Pipeline Masters) was not quite his best, but it was enough to guarantee he was the first Hawaiian invited to the Aussie tour.

Jeff flew down to Melbourne with Gerry Lopez and Reno Abellira in late March, 1974. They were met at the airport by Jack McCoy, a big, affable American surfer who had grown up on Oahu in the early 1960s and was now running a restaurant in the village of Torquay while he established himself as a surf photographer and moviemaker.

Says Jeff: "I remember thinking Torquay was kind of a funny place. The surf at Bells Beach looked pretty good, but it was really cold and the wind just went straight through you. I hadn't seen very much of England, but it seemed to me to have an English influence. People wore big thick pullovers and woollen beanies. They were very friendly, but real different.

"Jack introduced us to a surfer friend of his named Maurice Cole, a very young guy, powerfully built and with a real aura about him. Anyway, Maurice invited Gerry and Reno and me over to his place for a home-cooked meal one night. His girl, Anne, cooked a great meal and we enjoyed ourselves. Then when the meal was over, Maurice was out of the

Bells lineup.

room for some reason, and we just did the natural thing and started to help clear the plates away. Anne grabbed me by the shoulder and she said, in this real urgent voice, 'Don't do that, please don't do that'. It was weird, like way beyond being a good hostess. It was like, males just don't do that sort of thing in Australia."

Cole's driving technique also had Jeff baffled. "He was driving us down the Great Ocean Road to Lorne one day and it was like he really believed he was immortal. He'd pass five or six cars on a blind corner and laugh like crazy. I couldn't believe it, because I wasn't ready to die. But the more Maurice could see that I was scared, the crazier he drove."

When his own equipment proved unsuitable for the thick Bells waves, Jeff borrowed one of Peter Townend's boards in the contest and, although he finished out of the money in the main event, picked up two hundred dollars for the best nose ride. He fared little better in Sydney at the Coca Cola Surfabout, even when Paul Neilsen arrived with a couple of thicker, wider, small wave boards for him. Jeff recalls Reno Abellira looking at the stubby shapes and enquiring: "Do they bark?"

In Hawaii during 1973, Jeff had gravitated back to his old Punahou girlfriend Sandy Raymond, and as the Australian tour concluded, she flew out to join him. Jack McCoy had been filling Lopez and Jeff with stories of perfect, uncrowded surf on the Indonesian island of Bali, which had recently been made accessible by the construction of an international

Above: Monkey business in Bali, 1974.

Below: Bali crew 1974. Jeff centre, Bob McKnight left.

airport at Denpasar. The waves at a remote reef called Ulu Watu had been featured in two Australian surf movies, and McCoy had been so inspired by what he'd seen that he had spent much of the southern winter of '73 exploring the area.

"Ulu is only the beginning, man," he enthused. "There are perfect reef breaks everywhere over there, the living's cheap, the food's good, the weather's hot..."

Lopez and Hakman were sold. Gerry had teamed up with a Torquay girl, so when Sandy arrived, the five of them flew to Bali.

Says Jeff: "I remember flying in over the bay at Kuta and Jack pointed out Ulu Watu. It was just peeling off at what looked like about eight feet, no one out, the texture of the water kind of satiny and green, just beautiful. We checked into a little hotel called Arena Bungalows, and that afternoon we loosened up in real nice little waves at Kuta Reef, just along the beach from our hotel.

"The next morning we hit Ulu Watu. It was a long walk carrying our boards and equipment, and Jack got us lost. The tracks had apparently all changed since the previous year. But we finally got in there and it was five or six feet, medium tide, no one out. We climbed down through the cave and surfed it all day by ourselves. Gerry and I couldn't keep the smiles off our faces."

McCoy, Lopez and Hakman fell into a pattern of hitting Ulu Watu as soon after dawn as possible each morning, and surfing it until they dropped. But after a week of this, McCoy suggested that they delay their departure one morning and have breakfast with an American friend who had a small cottage on Jalan Pantai, the main Kuta Beach road.

As it turned out Sandy already knew Mike Boyum from his visits to Lahaina. Boyum was in his mid-thirties, about ten years older than Jeff and Gerry. He was quite new to surfing but he brought an athletic intensity to everything he did. He was extremely fit and committed to a macrobiotic diet, supplemented by vast quantities of sugar cane juice and blended magic mushrooms. Lopez, who had already gone through a heavy yoga phase with Dick Brewer, found him fascinating. Jeff was not so sure until Boyum blended up a heavy load of psychotropic mushrooms and poured bowls for everyone.

Some time later, Boyum said: "Hey Jeff, wanna see my trained ants?"

Jeff did the best he could, which was to nod once. Boyum led him into his small bedroom. Above the bed there was an army of ants cruising along the window sill. The ants were marching out of a tiny hole in the woodwork and proceeding in formation along the sill and up the other side of the window. Boyum said: "Watch this." He knocked twice on the wood with his knuckles. As one, the army of ants about-faced and marched back into the hole. Boyum slapped his hands together in glee. "Hot damn!" And went back to his blender to prepare seconds.

The mushroom smoothies became the mandatory start of every Ulu Watu day. Boyum joined them on the surf treks and, although he had no style and even less grace, Jeff noted that Michael Boyum was afraid of nothing. Jeff had carted a seven feet eight inch Brewer gun (his first Brewer in several years) around Australia with him without getting it wet. Boyum wanted it badly.

Says Jeff: "I told him it was really a Sunset board, but that didn't matter to Michael. He thought it was a beautiful board and he really wanted it, so I sold it to him. The next day we went around to his place real early and took our medicine, Gerry and me just a taste, Michael a whole shitload as usual. And driving out to Ulu I've got a real good buzz going. I look at Gerry and I can tell he's spinning too.

"We get out there and the surf is real good, about eight feet with bigger sets. We paddle out, no leashes. Maybe Gerry was using one. He'd just started to, I didn't like them. We're out there in the lineup and Boyum is paddling around totally loaded, giggling and carrying on. He takes off on this wave, about eight feet, and I remember seeing the red Brewer sliding down the face. Then he digs a rail and just clocks off. No style, no grace. We just hear this giggling as he goes down.

"So Boyum just disappears. Gerry and I are surfing away, having a ball. Maybe an hour goes by and we're getting just a little concerned. Then another hour, then we're like into the third hour! And suddenly he comes swimming along from the temple end of the reef, giggling away. I ask him where his board is, and he says it's in tiny little pieces. It got smashed against the cliff, he missed the cave and had to climb up the cliff way down the line, got harrassed by monkeys, backed around through the bush, missed the cave again, and here he is out in the lineup, about to swim for the cave again. He thought it was really funny. I couldn't believe it. I thought he should be dead!"

When Jeff got back to Hawaii it was almost summer. He'd been surfing all day every day for a month in a place that then seemed like the last frontier of civilisation. In 1974 there was nothing at Ulu Watu and very little at Kuta, particularly in the way of night life. So on his return to Oahu, Jeff felt uncharacteristically ready to let his hair down and party.

Since he and Felipe Pomar were about to start Dan Wallace's surf school for the summer, Jeff talked his room mate Bill Sickler into taking an apartment in town at the Colony Surf for the month of July. They were joined by a college buddy named Bob Hyman, and the trio embarked in earnest upon a party program.

Jeff in pensive mood, 1975.

Says Jeff: "It started out okay, but it degenerated. I'd teach surf from two to four in the afternoon, then we'd meet up and hit happy hour. By midnight we'd be howling, and we'd do some place like Nick's Fishmarket until dawn, then grab a few hours sleep, and try to wake up with a morning surf. Then maybe a nap, teach surf and start again. I'd never been much of a drinker, but for me the problem was that when I gave the lessons I'd start to feel okay, and then it'd be on again."

Jeff's flirtation with the booze-fuelled party life in Honolulu was short-lived. Suddenly it was September and there was just time for another hit on Bali before the North Shore winter. He caught a charter through Guam with Sickler and Hyman, checked into Arena Bungalows again and immediately launched into good surf at Ulu, Kuta Reef and a new spot in front of the luxury hotel strip at Sanur.

One day at Kuta Reef Jeff was joking around, having fun, when he noticed a serious, hawk-nosed fellow sitting very wide on a board about a foot longer than anyone else's. It reminded him of Buzzy Trent sitting wide in the lineup at Waimea Bay. He called out: "Hey Buzz, watcha doin' out there?"

The guy grinned. Soon he and Jeff were paddling for waves together. "Yours, Buzz, geev 'um, bra!" And the ginger-haired Californian was no slouch either. A goofy foot with a flowing style, he impressed Jeff with the calm unflappable way he surfed.

Jeff may not have known the guy he christened "Buzz", but Robert McKnight Jr certainly knew who Jeff was. A gremmie from Pasadena, Bob McKnight had grown up on a diet of surf movies and magazines. In his final college year he had attended the waterborne University Of The Seven Seas, stopping briefly at Bali. On graduation in '74, his first call had been to book an airline ticket back. McKnight was a serious surfer with track miles in Baja and beyond, but he was also serious about his future in business, and in subsequent conversations he impressed Jeff as a guy who had the right balance in his life. While Bob McKnight may have felt somewhat honoured that the famous surfer had picked him out as a friend, the reverse was also true.

The second Bali sojourn of 1974 ended on a bum note, literally. Jeff got a bad dose of Bali belly (as the local form of disyntery was known) and it intensified when he returned home. He went to several doctors but no one seemed able to identify the problem. Meanwhile, Jeff kept losing weight. Within six weeks he was down to one hundred and twenty pounds. He phoned his new buddy McKnight in California.

"Jesus, Jeff, you got problems! I just shat this thing!"

"No kidding, Buzz. You mean, like a tapeworm?"

"Jeff, this was no worm. This was a fucking snake!"

Right: Jeff with Florida surfer Jeff Crawford.

Below: Off the bottom at Waimea, Jeff and Terry Fitzgerald.

Opposite: Jeff and Reno, Waimea, 1973.

120

LeROY GRANNIS

CHAPTER 22

Monster takeoff at Waimea Bay. Smirnoff contest, 1974.

There hadn't been a spectacular winter on the North Shore since 1969. No one knew about the El Nino effect yet, but the consensus amongst the big wave veterans was that a monster swell was overdue.

"Don't worry," said Peter Cole, sitting out back of his little A-frame at Rocky Point, "It will come. They always come."

Jeff believed him, and when Sunset started to rise during the afternoon before the commencement of the Smirnoff waiting period, he felt that something serious was coming. Jeff surfed until dark, and the last few sets of the day were more regular and more powerful than they had been all day. It was solid and rising, and Jeff anticipated good fifteen feet waves the following day. For him this was perfect. He had the boards (Brewers again), he had the experience, and he was ready.

Jeff slept uneasily up on Pupukea Highlands that night, and was up before first light, peering through the sliding doors at the open ocean. From the house the view of Waimea was obstructed, but you could normally see the swell pattern at Laniakea. On this morning, however, a heavy sea mist clung to the high ground, restricting vision. Jeff opened the doors and went outside. There was a roar as if someone had built a power plant next door during the night. Jeff couldn't believe his ears. On a big swell he had sometimes heard the roar of the surf if the wind was still, but this was ridiculous! He dressed quickly, ate some fruit and put his eight feet six inch Brewer gun on the roof of his bug.

He drove as fast as the bends would allow down the Pupukea road, then almost drove off the edge at the final U-bend, where there was an unobstructed view of the ocean. He jammed on the brakes and looked out to sea. Holy fucking shit! Jeff had never seen anything like it. Open ocean reefs he didn't even know about were going off all over the place. The lines of swell were stacked to the horizon like corduroy. There was very little wind and the surface of the ocean was quite smooth, accentuating the enormity of the waves. It was beyond big – words failed Jeff – and it was perfect.

Smirnoff '74.

He swung the little car around and drove back up the hill. Bill Sickler had a nine feet Brewer gun which Jeff had used before. It was too short but it was the best thing they had. He woke his room mate. "Bill, Bill, gimme your gun!"

"Duh, what?"

"Your nine footer, I need it. Can I borrow it?"

"What, yeah, take the fucker. What time is it?"

Jeff was off down the hill again. He parked at Waimea and took the board off quickly and quietly.

He recalls: "It was clean and immaculate and, well, Waimea never gets too big if it's clean. Maybe once every ten years. I didn't really look, you know. There was no one around, it's only just light, so I ran down to the shorebreak, waited for my chance and paddled out. What was going through my mind was, I'm fit and ready for this contest, if I get a few waves in before it I'll know the conditions, I'll know where to sit and I'll win. I figured it was maybe twenty-five feet on the sets. It was big, but I knew big and I could handle it, and this go-out would give me the edge I needed."

As he paddled out Jeff realised that there was a lot of ocean moving around. He sat on the outside boil and waited for a set. The first one that came through was the biggest he'd ever seen.

"I paddled over the first two, then turned around and snagged the third. The drop went on forever. I got a little bit of air, but I held on, reached the bottom and got the hell out of there. Made it. Great feeling. That's the deal at Waimea. If you're out there with no crowd, you can pick your line, set it all up, then you've got maybe an eighty per cent chance of making the thing, if you get to the bottom. You sort of know the score as you drop down the face, only then it's too late to do anything.

"So I paddled out again and got another one a little bigger, maybe twenty-five plus. I made that one too, and now I started to feel really confident. Like I'm cookin'! I paddle out again and sit on the boil, then suddenly the horizon goes black. I was sitting so far out I could see up the coast towards Sunset and I could see this set just wrapping. The wave you ride at Waimea Bay is just the tail end of a freight train that shoots right along the entire North Shore, creating havoc and destruction, and from out there I could see it coming along the whole coastline. And it was totally horrifying.

"I started paddling for open ocean, paddling for my life. When I made it up the face of the first one, I looked over my shoulder before I dropped into the trough and I was in open ocean. When the first wave subsided I looked around again and the whole bay was white water. I put my head down and kept paddling over four or five more. I'd already had the biggest wave of my life out here, and these waves were at least ten feet bigger!"

When the ocean settled down again, Jeff paddled into the normal lineup and waited. When a smaller set came through he caught another wave and made it. He had been back at the boil for about fifteen minutes when Sam Hawk paddled out.

"Yo, Jeff! It's good, huh! I saw your last wave, man. How often do those sets come through?"

Jeff said: "Sammy, that's not a set. That's a lull!"

"No waaaay, man!"

Mike Miller was next to paddle out. He waved to Jeff but paddled deeper inside, out of earshot. Just as he got settled, another throbbing set began its approach. Jeff and Sammy Hawk stroked for the horizon, with Miller way behind them. They scratched over one, two, three...then no Miller. The naked hotdogger of Hossegor was gone.

Jeff and Hawk moved back into the lineup and finally caught sight of Miller, swimming along the cliff-line, trying to avoid the killer rip. They both caught a wave, then looked around to see Miller swimming back out into the lineup.

Jeff said: "Mike, what the hell are you doing out here?"

"Missed the beach. Gotta try again."

The import of what he was saying took a while for Jeff to comprehend. Miller was one of the most experienced watermen on the North Shore. If he couldn't get in, no one could get in. Jeff estimated the size of the killer sets at somewhere between thirty and thirty-five feet, which was pretty much close-out size for Waimea Bay. When the surf reached these proportions, the amount of water rushing into the small bay was so great that each out-going wave effectively drained the beach, creating an all-powerful surge of water in a west-erly direction, towards the notorious Waimea shorebreak in the middle of the beach. If you were swimming and the surge got you, the only chance you had was to head for open ocean and try again.

Mike Miller appeared in the lineup a second time. "Fuckin' hay! Missed it again."

Jeff said: "You okay, Mike?"

"Yeah, yeah. I'll give it another fuckin' try."

He swam into the impact zone again for another head clearing. Jeff had had five good waves and judged it time to head in. The next set that came through, he picked off the sec-ond, a clean twenty-five footer. Jeff made it and just as the wave backed into deeper water, he jammed a cutback and proned out, paddling as hard as he could back into the impact zone. This, he knew, was the secret at maximum Waimea. The wave tossed him around like a cork, but he held on and kept in line with the cliff, well away from the savage rip. Then, right before the shorebreak, he kicked his board away and let the ten feet surge hurl him onto the beach.

Up in the car park, contest director Fred Hemmings was conferring in hushed tones with the sponsors, the television crew and the emergency services men. Hemmings felt the contest couldn't go ahead. It was too big, lives would be endangered. Jeff was asked his opinion.

"Well," he said, "I think it's peaked. I think it's on its way down."

Hemmings and the others looked to sea again and saw that Jeff was probably right. There were now a half-dozen surfers in the water, and they hadn't been troubled by a close-out set for at least thirty minutes. In all probability, the monster swell had peaked some time before dawn at forty feet plus. When Jeff had first paddled out, there were perhaps two sets of thirty-five feet waves. Now it had settled at a consistent twenty-five to thirty feet. It was probably about ten feet bigger than any contested surf in the the history of the sport, and several of the competitors were all-rounders who had never surfed waves half this size. Hemmings took a very big gulp and called the 1974 Smirnoff on.

It was the most extraordinary surfing contest of all time. Some invitees simply refused to paddle out. Others sat in the lineup and declined to take a wave. The surf roared up over the road at Laniakea, and there was a day-long traffic jam as five thousand people made their way to standing room only Waimea. Some said it wasn't a surfing contest, that it was about something else, but perhaps it was both. Terry Fitzgerald remembers paddling out with Gerry Lopez to start the semi finals. As an enormous set loomed, Lopez said: "If Hakman yells mother, we paddle in".

For safety reasons (allegedly) a water patrol of seasoned North Shore veterans sat outside the lineup all day, marshalling heats and ensuring that no one swimming was in trouble. The patrol included Jose Angel, Peter Cole, Ricky Grigg and a young wannabe big wave rider from Hanalei Bay, known as T-Bone. How T-Bone got into the water patrol, no one knew for sure (some said he was a protege of Cabell's) but he loved his work.

When Jeff hit the water in the first semi-final, he and Reno, James Jones, Buzzy Kerbox, Brad McCaul and a couple of others, were corralled just outside the zone while the previous heat dispersed and the water patrolmen caught a wave or two each. Jose Angel and Peter Cole both got the first wave of a good-sized set, with Ricky Grigg on the next. Jeff and the others watched as the patrol surfers got their jollies. Then they looked seaward as the last and biggest wave approached. Jeff judged it nearly thirty feet. T-Bone was in the zone. The semi-finalists hooted nervously as the kid from Hanalei started stroking for it.

Says Jeff: "The wave just jacked and it was huge. It started to suck him up the face and he was at that moment of commitment. We were all so close we could see the expression on his face. He just faltered in his paddling rhythm for a split second and I could tell he was wondering. Then Peter and Jose are paddling out and they're yelling at him to go, go! Suddenly we're yelling too, and he's committed. I'll never forget that look on his face, a mixture of apprehension and pride. I mean, what's he gonna do? Every surfer in the world that he respects and admires is watching him. Suddenly he's hanging there in space, and at that moment he knew he wasn't going to make it. He just plunged, fell out of the sky, landed on his board and the both of them got sucked back up over the falls again. There was a split second where he knew he wasn't going to make that wave and where he could have pulled back, but he didn't. It was a beautiful act of bravery and commitment.

"That wave of T-Bone's is probably the single most electrifying thing I've ever seen in surfing, because for me it just captures the whole deal. He pushed it too far, but he knew he had to or it wasn't worth a damn thing."

The second semi-final produced the surfing of the day, with Jeff and Reno Abellira going head to head on the biggest waves ever ridden for points.

Says Jeff: "Reno was just brilliant. He was taking off on big waves and getting airborne down the face. As soon as he landed, he'd just jam the thing into the pit, bury the rail and

The biggest waves ever contested, Waimea, 1974.

do this big, winding turn. I even saw his feet leave the board on one takeoff! In my view he was the surfer of the day in that semi, you just couldn't surf Waimea any better than that. But in the final, I thought I traded places with Reno and surfed above myself. Everything just came together and I surfed way beyond my limits. On one twenty-five feet wave I was screaming down the face and the nose of the board was suddenly level with the tail. I had to press down on my heels to straighten it. This was a real tribute to Brewer, because on a lesser board I was gone for sure."

The contest Jeff still calls the most exciting of his career, came down to half a point difference between him and Reno, and Reno got the nod. Three judges placed Reno first, two in second and one in third. Jeff was scored first by two, tied for first by another, second by two, and tied for second by the third judge. Under the subjective judging system, no result could have been closer.

First love, Sunset, 1974.

CHAPTER 23

Laniakea, 1973.

During the preliminary heats of the 1974 Duke Invitational, held in twelve feet waves at Sunset, Jeff loaned a board to his friend Paul Neilsen. Neilsen was having all kinds of equipment problems, but Jeff reassured him: "Paul, this board is special".

Indeed it was. Neilsen caught two spectacular waves before wiping out on a third that was equally spectacular. The board drifted into the savage rip and, pushed along by a strong offshore wind, disappeared out to sea. That was the end of the Magic Board.

Like most surfers of the modern era, Jeff owned hundreds of boards during his competitive career, some of them dogs, some of them truly works of art. But the seven feet eleven inch Brewer pintail that Jeff called his Magic Board was the best of them all. He had to fight to own it, and when he finally sold it he had to lease it back. "It was simply one in a million", he recalls.

The story of the Magic Board dated back to Christmas 1972, when Jeff and Dick Brewer were getting back together again after a couple of years' break in their long-standing shaper/test pilot relationship. There were several reasons for the split, none of them personal. One was that Jeff had gone to work for Plastic Fantastic in Huntington Beach in 1969. By the time he got back on track in Hawaii in 1970, Brewer was in such demand that there was an impossibly long wait for a board. (At the time it was said that you had to be a Peruvian to get a board immediately.)

Jeff experimented with a number of shapers, like Jim Gardner, but late in 1972 he was gravitating back towards Brewer. On Christmas Eve Brewer sealed the deal by presenting him with a beautiful nine feet six inch gun with a superbly-drawn, thinned out tail. It was the ideal speed machine for maximum Sunset, where Jeff excelled.

Jeff recalls: "I loved the thing and I started riding it at Sunset at all sizes. One eight feet day I was out there with Greg Tucker, and I was so stoked in my board I insisted he try it out. So I hopped on the board he was riding, a seven eleven. I swung it around and took off on a real steep one, thinking as I stood up that I wasn't going to make it. I remember

Jeff at Sunset, 1974.

thinking how stupid I was, because I'd have to swim in and bring the board back out for Greg. But the board made the drop perfectly, and then it did everything I asked of it. It was just magic! A little bit thicker and wider than the standard board, it just seemed more responsive than anything I'd ever ridden. Afer a few waves I paddled up to Greg Tucker and told him I had to have it."

But Tucker had bad news. The magic Brewer was not his. It belonged to Jack Reeves, Brewer's glasser who had the best collection of surfboards on the North Shore, perhaps in the world. Reeves had an eye for a perfect shape, and when Brewer had outdone himself, he knew before he glassed it. In this case, Brewer had built the board for David Nuuhiwa, then offered it to him at cost price. When Nuuhiwa politely explained that he did not pay for surfboards, that people paid him to ride them, Reeves grabbed the board for himself.

Jeff went to see Jack Reeves. "Jack, please let me buy the board. I'll pay you anything you want, I've gotta have the board."

"Sorry, Jeff, it's not for sale."

Jeff went to see Brewer. "Dick, I gotta have that board. Make Jack sell it to me."

"Relax, Jeff. You like that board, I'll make you one exactly the same."

But no two Brewers were ever the same, and the seven eleven he made Jeff was better, Brewer said. He'd refined it here a little, fine tuned it there just a bit. But it didn't have the magic. Finally Jeff talked Brewer into making Reeves an offer he couldn't refuse – two boards for the one. Reeves took the bait and Jeff took the Magic Board.

Jeff and the Magic Board were inseparable for the rest of the winter. He rode it in waves ranging from four feet to twenty feet and could never fault it. But somehow during the off-season the gloss went off the Magic Board, and when he came to review his equipment for the 1973-74 winter, he discarded it and sold it to a friend named Joey Smoot. He had new boards from Brewer and from a new shaper on the North Shore named Tom Parrish, but nothing could replace the Magic Board. Before the contest season began, Jeff went cap in hand to Joey Smoot and offered to buy it back at more than he had paid for it. Smoot said no, however he would lease it to Jeff for a percentage of his prize money. He had Jeff over a barrel. Jeff leased the board back and rode it to a second placing in the Smirnoff at Laniakea, a third in the Duke at Sunset and a fourth in the Pipeline Masters. Smoot's lease deal was immediately lucrative. But with the season nearing an end, Jeff managed to negotiate a purchase price.

In February he rode the Magic Board to his second successive victory in the Hang Ten American Pro in perfect twelve feet Sunset waves. He recalls: "I just couldn't do any wrong. I'd be paddling up the face of these things, then just swing around and drop down the face sideways and still make it. I think it was the best I ever surfed in a contest at Sunset, except perhaps for the first Duke."

The statistics bear him out. In the final, Jeff amassed an incredible nine hundred and sixty-six points to finish almost three hundred and fifty ahead of second placegetter Jimmy Lucas.

The Magic Board was looking a little worse for wear by this, and Jeff decided to save it from the rigours of life on the road. He didn't take it on the 1974 Australia or Bali trips, but kept it for one last season on the North Shore. As it turned out, he couldn't ride it in the monster Smirnoff at Waimea, and on its last outing at Sunset, Paul Neilsen lost the Magic Board at sea.

Says Jeff: "I wasn't too happy when that happened, but it wasn't Paul's fault, and it seemed like an appropriate end. The old girl just drifted off peacefully, rather than getting ground into the reef bit by bit."

The 1974 Duke was memorable in ways other than the demise of the Magic Board. Two days before the event Jeff had been fooling around on his acreage at Pupukea with a horse owned by Cindy Jacobs (not her real name), his new room mate. Cindy was the girlfriend of a North Shore surfer who had just been busted on drugs charges in Peru. With him indisposed, she needed a roof over her head, but she came with a horse called Boy. Since Jeff and Bill Sickler had an acre of land, they agreed to take her in.

But Jeff didn't like horses. "Come on, Jeff," said Cindy, "He's the most beautiful horse, aren't you Boy. Come and sit on him for a bit."

Cindy led the horse right up to the driveway next to the house and Jeff placed his left foot tentatively in the stirrups and tried to mount. Boy reared up in fright and his hind legs slipped on the concrete. The horse came crashing down on Cindy, catching Jeff's leg in the process. Jeff had broken a bone in his foot, but Cindy, whose slender frame bore the brunt of the horse's weight, had serious pelvic damage and was hospitalised for almost two months.

Jeff's injury may have been slight compared to Cindy's but it was extremely painful. He could not put any weight on the foot and looked certain to miss the Duke. He asked the doctor if there was a painkiller that might do the trick, and was told that there was a new drug which was still being tested for side effects. The doctor reluctanty prescribed it with a severe warning to use it sparingly.

The night before the Duke, Jeff was still in agony. Paul Neilsen had suggested they go to a party in Honolulu. "Yeah, why not? I certainly can't surf."

Jeff dropped another painkiller on the way into town, then enjoyed a few beers. Around eleven he noticed he could walk without pain. He put some pressure on the foot and felt nothing. He hurriedly found Neilsen. "Paul, let's get out of here. I'm okay!"

Bernie Baker's lanai overlooking Sunset, 1975.

Above: Jeff and Paul Neilsen at Duke Boyd's home in the Rockies, 1974.

Below: Jeff at Burleigh Heads.

Loaded on painkillers, Jeff surfed conservatively but consistently for a third in the Duke, then crashed for twelve hours. When he woke up the next day, he was crippled again.

With the contest season over, Jeff and Paul Neilsen flew to Aspen, Colorado, for a couple of weeks' skiing at the invitation of Duke Boyd and his wife, Brenda. When Jeff returned to the North Shore, Cindy was just about to get out of hospital. He felt somehow responsible for her injury, and took it upon himself to play nurse. He found he kind of liked Cindy's spark, and a relationship developed.

When it came time to go to Australia at the end of March, Jeff invited Cindy along. Although the Bells Beach Classic was the first contest of the tour, they flew not to Melbourne but to Adelaide, the city at the edge of Australia's great southern desert and home base of John Arnold, the Australian licensee for Golden Breed. Arnold was a straight-shooting businessman who had turned the Golden Breed label into a huge success in Australia. Over dinner in Adelaide he wrote Jeff a fat cheque and explained exactly what he wanted him to do.

While Queenslander Michael Peterson had begun to make such a ferocious attack on the objective "points for manoeuvres" judging system that he looked unstoppable, at least in Australia, Jeff's incredible competitive record in Hawaii still enabled his sponsors to legitimately claim him as professional surfing's "world champion". To capitalise on this, Arnold's marketing machine had put together what amounted to a personal appearance tour, taking in the major cities of Australia's eastern seaboard. When Gerry Lopez flew in a day or so later, the two embarked on a round of media interviews and appearances in Adelaide, Melbourne, Sydney and Brisbane.

Although he was always thoroughly professional in his dealings with sponsors, Jeff was never comfortable in the promotional role, and when he got to Brisbane he almost walked away from the whole deal. A local surf movie distributor had put together a night of surf movies and rock music with the star attraction being "Jeff Hakman Live On Stage". In fact on those rare occasions when Jeff had actually been on stage he had died. This night was no exception.

Jeff recalls: "The place was full of people, maybe two thousand, and they were having a ball until I got up on stage. The movie guy's got a microphone and I've got one, and he's asking me questions about ding repairs. Ding repairs? Like what am I supposed to say? Yeah, every night I mix up a hot batch, then sand them down all nice and smooth so my board's ready for the next morning! It was the most embarrassing moment of my life, and there have been a few. I'm thinking, how can I just quietly slip off this stage?"

Back in Melbourne for the Bells meet, Jeff and Cindy were met at the airport and driven to Torquay by a young Melbourne journalist named Harry Hodge. Hodge and some friends had just started a surfing magazine, and acting as chauffeur provided an opportunity for an in-depth interview with the man people were calling "Mr Sunset". It was the start of a friendship which would play a major role in the lives of both men.

During the North Shore winter of 1974, Jeff had been introduced to yet another Australian, surfboard builder Geoff McCoy, who had some progressive small board shapes and a team of very good young surfers riding them. One day at Sunset Jeff had watched Bruce Raymond, one of the "McCoy Boys", take off behind the peak and carve a flowing bottom turn to make the wave. That evening he sought out the young surfer (making his day) to examine his board. Jeff subsequently tried some of McCoy's short boards and struck a deal to ride them in the Australian contests.

Says Jeff: "It had reached the point where there was enough money at stake on beach break contests that you had to have specialised boards. Our Hawaiian boards really worked best in our conditions. Guys like McCoy knew what was needed for Australia."

Michael Peterson flung himself all over the flat face of the Bells waves to easily win the event, but Jeff, riding a six feet seven inch McCoy swallowtail, finished a creditable third, the best finish by a foreigner in an Australian pro contest to that time.

The real action, however, was on the social scene, where Maurice Cole continued his education of Jeff in the matter of social graces Down Under. Jack McCoy hosted an eating competition at his restaurant, and Cole chowed down in the final against fellow Australian surfers Rabbit Bartholomew and Ian Cairns. Both Bartholomew and Cairns were prodigious eaters, but no one could match Cole in matters of gluttony. Jeff watched in amazement as Maurice quaffed almost his own body weight in enchiladas, kept it in until the final bell, then staggered off to relieve himself.

Says Jeff: "It was real interesting. I was starting to get a handle on the Torquay male thing".

But if Torquay and Bells Beach weren't exactly Jeff's speed, Queensland's Gold Coast was. After competing with little luck in the Coca Cola Surfabout in Sydney, Jeff flew to the Gold Coast to join Paul Neilsen on his home turf. Neilsen had been telling him about Burleigh Heads' famous barrels for three years now, and the day he arrived he saw them at their finest. In fact, Jeff had arrived at the beginning of the longest and cleanest swell ever experienced in that part of the world. For twenty-three record-breaking days, the tubes kept winding off at Burleigh and Kirra Point.

Says Jeff: "It was five feet one day, six feet the next. It just kept coming. I thought it must be like this all the time and I just wanted to move there right away. One day I was talking to some one on the lawn at Burleigh, and I saw Paul disappear behind the curtain. I kept talking for a while longer, then I looked back and he popped out the other end. It was just incredible, and Neilsen, Rabbit and Peterson were just going off. Towards the end we were just wrecks, praying every day that it would go flat."

DICK HOOLE

Above: *Jeff at Burleigh.*
Below: *Kirra — the 23-day swell.*

DICK HOOLE

CHAPTER 24

Uluwatu lineup.

The word was out about Bali. When Jeff and Cindy got there in the middle of May, the village of Kuta was teeming with both major and bit players on the international surf scene. While there were some pro tour surfers, like Jeff, working out between contests, by far the greater number were travelling soul surfers, those people of mysterious means who seemed (and still do) to bob up on Maui or Mauritius, Hossegor or Hanalei Bay, Kuta or Cactus, wherever there is a chance of a surf and the certainty of a constant supply of recreational drugs. The players have been on the scene since the scene began.

Before she had moved in with Jeff and Bill Sickler, Cindy had moved in some culturally diverse company for a sweet young thing from Long Beach, California. She had contact with heroin users, for example, but in the six months he had known her, Jeff had never seen her use the drug. His own drug use had actually tapered off dramatically since he'd hit his straps as a pro surfer, and heroin was something that repulsed him. Coke? On a party night, sure, why not? But heroin, that was the stuff that the guys down at San Pedro always ended up on, the guys that his father had warned him about all those years ago.

The Bali underground scene in 1975 was brimming with heroin, high quality and cheap. While Jeff was spending his days out surfing perfect ten feet Sanur, others in the scene were experimenting with heroin. Cindy was coy about her dabbling at first, but when Jeff's Australian and Hawaiian surfing buddies produced their own stashes and started smoking the stuff through foil, it came out into the open.

Jeff: "I remember smoking it for the first time and asking, what's this stuff supposed to do? Like I was always up for experimenting with drugs, but heroin? Whoa, that was a bit too scary. Anyway, I smoked it and I remember this hammer hitting my spinal column and a warm rush come through my whole system. Hashish, LSD, cocaine, magic mushrooms, you name it, I'd tried it. But I can honestly say that no drug had even come close to making this kind of impression on me. I wouldn't say I was hooked, just like that, but by the time we left Bali I had a nice little habit going."

DICK HOOLE

Although in the past he'd been involved in three hashish and marijuana smuggling operations (two of them failures), Jeff had drawn a very clear line in the sand when it came to the moral justification of his actions. These were drugs that didn't harm anyone. Heroin was a different story. But the insidious effects of this most insidious of drugs do not take long to manifest themselves, and after just a month of daily use, it seemed perfectly natural to Jeff that, rather than run out of supply, they would simply smuggle a couple of ounces back into Hawaii.

Cindy came through customs with two ounces of Penang rocks inserted in her, and so hungry for a hit were they that they grabbed a rental car and drove straight to a Waikiki hotel. Happily loaded again, they began to plot how they could get through the summer on only seventy grams.

The summer surf school was a blast. Literally. Jeff would have a big hit instead of lunch and just cruise through the afternoon, pushing kids onto waves and showing them where they were going wrong.

Says Jeff: "Physically I was in great shape, so the fact that I might skip a meal or not look after myself properly didn't have an immediate effect. And there's a myth about people on drugs being unreliable. It's drug users who haven't got drugs who are unreliable. We had drugs coming out our ears, so I showed up on time every day. No problem."

But by the end of August the rocks had run out. Realising that the party had to end at some stage, Jeff went through a withdrawal, something he would come to know in drugs-peak as "jonesing". The physical withdrawal that first time was not particularly painful, but it was a psychological nightmare.

"It was just very difficult to come to terms with the fact that I had an addiction. Suddenly I saw the world in a completely new light, the barriers were down, I suppose."

Trying to snap out of it, Jeff and Cindy took a trip to Baja in the fall. Jeff recalls: "In Baja I'd be out surfing and I started to notice that even then I'd be thinking about heroin. I wouldn't be sitting out there thinking about the next wave, I'd be thinking about the next hit, imagining the rush."

Finally, as winter approached Jeff managed to break the shackles of his dependency and to concentrate on his preparation for the contest season. It helped that it was a good winter. Fledgling Mark Richards won an Aussie-dominated Smirnoff (again completed in big Waimea) but Jeff finished a strong fourth and followed up with a third in the Duke. But it was the free surfing that captured most attention. It was the year of the Aussie assault. Richards, Rabbit Cairns, and of course South Africa's Tomson playing to the gallery at Off The Wall or, on bigger days, Pipeline. But the west swell kept pouring in and Jeff surfed almost every day in the smaller crowd at Sunset.

By the end of the winter he was superbly fit, surfing at his peak, and the silliness of the summer seemed like a long time ago. Except that sometimes he'd be sitting in the lineup, and he'd start thinking about that warm, wonderful rush.

Jeff had Tom Parrish build him a couple of bigger boards to take to Bells Beach in '76, just in case the Easter surf lived up to its reputation for size and power. As he watched Parrish putting the finishing touches on a seven feet two inch board, Jeff suddenly had a flash of inspiration. He told the shaper: "I want a real thick fin on that sucker, hollowed out in the middle to keep the weight down".

Jeff simply took the fin home with him and brought it back a few days later with three ounces of cocaine inside it. It was duly glassed on and it flew to Australia with Jeff, Barry Kanaiaupuni, Cindy and her friend Shirley Rogers.

Jeff wasn't much interested in cocaine, but he knew that it would fetch top dollar in Australia where, coincidentally, heroin was relatively cheap. It was a ridiculous risk to take, especially given the interest the DEA had taken in him some years earlier, but it made perfect sense to Jeff. He says: "If it meant scoring heroin, then it made sense. Even after having a clean act all winter, that was still the way one part of my brain worked."

Honolua Bay, 1976.

Jeff with Paul Neilsen at Torquay, 1976. More flash than cash.

Above and below: Hakman and Peterson, wild-eyed and hard to beat in 1976.

Not only did Jeff have clean-living, hard-working family man Barry Kanaiaupuni as an unknowing accomplice on this scam, but at Sydney Airport they were met by Geoff McCoy, at that time the only person in Australian surfing who was more vocally anti-drug than the Neilsen brothers.

While Cindy and Shirley Rogers flew straight on to Queensland, Jeff and Barry travelled with McCoy to his factory on the New South Wales central coast, where Jeff unpacked his Parrishes and recoiled in mock horror when he saw the fat fin on the seven two.

"Jesus!" he said, "I can't believe what Tom's done here. Look at the foil on this fin. Ridiculous! It's gotta go." He set the board up in a bay and quickly sanded the offending fin off, depositing it in his bag. Team rider Bruce Raymond was deputised to put a new fin on, and as soon as he had taken delivery of his short boards shaped by McCoy, Jeff was on his way back to the airport.

Jeff and the girls rented an apartment overlooking the surf at Kirra and Jeff fell into a pattern of surfing two or three times a day between snorting sessions. The hottest performer in the water was, of course, Michael Peterson, fresh from a season in Hawaii where he had firmly established a reputation as the fastest surfer and biggest hassler alive. One day at Sunset he had offended veteran Hawaiian Ben Aipa so much that Aipa had seen Peterson's board washing in on the beach, and he had strolled down from the car park and snapped the fin off as the Australian swam helplessly shoreward.

Says Jeff: "It was hard to tell with Michael whether he was just naturally rude or totally focused on himself to the exclusion of everyone else. He just saw the wave, and he had to have it."

At Kirra, back in his element, Peterson was coming out of the tube, carving a figure eight, then slotting back into it as though he had never left. Michael Peterson was probably at the peak of his surfing ability that Australian autumn, a surfer as naturally gifted as Nat Young. But he was also, like Jeff, the victim of his own social environment. Their preference was for different poisons, but both Jeff and Michael were locked into the pleasure principle and found ways to assist each other.

The party program had already eaten into Jeff's coke stash considerably, but he left Kirra for Melbourne with two ounces of heroin and an ounce of cocaine. The world's leading professional surfer set up house in Torquay, where he proceeded to get loaded every morning, then go out and surf near his best.

It's strange how the dice roll. Jeff Hakman was twenty-six years old and for four years he had been widely accepted as the best surfer in the world, although all that was about to change. Peterson had proven that he was even better than Jeff at the points-for-manoeuvres game, and moves were afoot to establish a real world tour with a cumulative points championship, thus taking the accent off the North Shore big wave meets. Jeff knew that his days at the top of the pile in surfing were numbered. His life had to take a new direction. The problem was that two directions were fighting for supremacy.

A year earlier, when he had borrowed a pair of boardshorts at Narrabeen Beach in Sydney and had fleetingly glimpsed the future, Jeff could not have foreseen that something as crazy as a pinkish-white powder heated on a piece of foil, would stand between him and his ambition, but it was about to. And as he prepared for the Bells meet by imbibing huge quantities of drugs, something snapped inside Jeff's head. It was a crazy thing, but he simply stopped worrying, and let nature run its course.

The first effect of this was that he won the contest, becoming the first non-Australian to do so. The meet was interminable, held over four rounds interrupted by changes of venue and flat days. Jeff was fucked up for a lot of it, hiding a multitude of sins behind dark glasses, but he surfed the system, got an early lead and held onto it. Considering the fact that it was to be his last victory in one of the most remarkable winning runs in the history of surfing, it was something of a let-down. But considering the drugged out state Jeff was in at the time, it was also a minor miracle.

The second effect was that the cocktail of drugs and celebratory booze instilled in Jeff a totally manic, go-for-it approach to life. He hit the parties with a vengeance. One evening he found himself in the wee small hours with one of Torquay's more notorious bon vivants. They drove around the town crushing phone booths and popping tent ropes in the camping ground.

The third effect was that, in the contradictory way of these things, he focused through the haze on the one thing he wanted, and he decided he would not leave Torquay until he had it.

During the Coca Cola Surfabout of 1975, Jeff had found himself light a pair of trunks one day at Narrabeen. Australian surfer Mark Warren loaned him a pair of his, which fitted better than any Jeff had ever worn before. They had scalloped legs and a contrasting wide waistband, and they seemed to sit perfectly on the hips. Since 1950s California when he had put up with the discomfort of wet and heavy baggies, Jeff had always been conscious of the importance of trunks that felt right, and they were a rare thing. These felt right. He took note of the label, Quiksilver, and then he forgot to give them back.

The following winter in Hawaii the Lightning Bolt surfboard label became established with Gerry Lopez as its icon. On Gerry's instigation, label manager Jack Shipley began importing Quiksilver shorts to sell in the Bolt shop in Honolulu. Every time Jeff dropped in to see Shipley, he had just sold out of Quiksilvers.

So when business major Bob McKnight cruised into Hawaii to stay with Jeff at Pupukea in February 1976, their discussions between surf sessions centred on how they might get in on the rapidly growing surf industry.

Jeff pointed to the wave label on his shorts. "This is the key," he told McKnight.

Jeff can't remember at what point in the 1976 Bells campaign he approached Quiksilver boss Alan Green about procuring a manufacturing licence for the USA – Jeff can't remember a lot of things about that Easter – but at some point before the meet was concluded, Green and his partners, John Law and Brewster Everett, took Jeff to see their tiny production facility in what Jeff recalls as "a converted chicken run". Certainly it was still very much a cottage industry after six years, but the down-to-earth Australians had come up with a pair of shorts that the world of surfing wanted. Now all they had to do was market them.

Jeff nodded his head knowingly while Green explained the quality of the fibre, the cut of the cloth, the special kind of Velcro fly, the unique stud. The Australians are serious, Jeff thought. They know what they're doing. Do I?

Negotiations were suspended for days at a time for reasons of surf or Jeff getting loaded, but Jeff kept coming back to Alan Green with his basic licence proposal. Finally, they met over dinner at the height of the contest madness. Many bottles of wine were consumed before Jeff was moved to cry, in exasperation: "Alan, for fuck's sake, I am totally committed to making Quiksilver successful in the United States. What do I have to do to show that to you?"

Jeff looked around the table and plucked a heavy decorative paper cloth from the centre. "Do you want me to eat this doily?"

Alan Green lit a cigarette and looked down his nose at Jeff. He grinned and nodded. Jeff grabbed the doily and started shoving it into his mouth. He nearly gagged as he chewed it up and slowly digested it, but Green was delighted.

When Jeff had finished, Alan Green stood up and bellowed. "Okay Hakman, you win! Take the fucking licence."

The lawyers and accountants had worked out an agreement in principle before Jeff had recovered his appetite.

Above: *Lightning Bolt crew – Shipley, Russell, Lopez and Fat Paul.*

Below: *Bells champion with Rory Russell and friends.*

CHAPTER 25

Right and opposite: Frames from Band On The Run, *1976-77.*
Jeff at work and play.

Jeff had the Quiksilver licence. He had his new direction. The rest of the Australian tour was a complete blur. He remembers being driven to the airport for the flight home by Thor Svensen, an American-born Sydney school teacher who had once been the head of the prestigious Windansea Surf Club in California.

Svenson had seen the demise through drugs of many of his youthful stars of the 1960s, but it cannot have occurred to him that Jeff Hakman, sitting in animated conversation in the passenger seat opposite him, was about to degenerate into a dribbling mess and shiver in the foetal position in an airline seat for twelve hours, then hide away until his demons had moved on.

For Jeff, however, this had become the normal pattern of life. And just as he was able in Victoria to concurrently win a major surfing contest, do the biggest business deal of his life and stay fucked up throughout, so he was able to chatter away to his old friend Thor, then jones it out over the Pacific through the endless night.

The master of Sunset Beach had become the master of deception, the perfect closet junkie.

But it was worse than he could have imagined. For two months he and Cindy had been doing upwards of a gram a day. Jeff would wake in the night with the cold sweats and fix himself up a little something, then go back to bed. Sometimes twice a night. By the time they had driven from Honolulu Airport to Pupukea, Jeff had been hanging out for almost eighteen hours. While Buzz McKnight slept soundly in the next room, Jeff crawled up the walls.

He recalls: "I'd never felt so bad in my life. It was so bad that I really thought I should see someone. I just didn't think I could make it through. Then, just when it's getting really bad, Cindy's there, holding a little bag."

Cindy had once again made use of nature's own smuggling compartment to bring in the leftovers of the the long Australian binge. Jeff had been so screwed up most of the tour that he had no idea how great or small their intake had been, and Cindy had successfully squirrelled away seven or eight grams, enough to wean them off.

Within a couple of days Jeff was up to speaking to his prospective business partner, Bob McKnight, who had been waiting patiently for Jeff to recover from his "jet lag". Jeff had phoned from Australia with two lots of good news, that he had won the Bells contest and that Alan Green had agreed to give him the Quiksilver licence for the United States. But that had been weeks earlier, and McKnight's enthusiasm for the task ahead was tempered by two things; the first was that he couldn't really see a business future in the surf industry, the second was that the only thing he knew about the garment industry was that while some people made shirts, a hell of a lot lost them.

"The rag trade!" his father had laughed down the phone. "You got the wrong kind of name for starters!"

McKnight's career plan had been to work through the summer waiting tables, then return to the University of Southern California in September to complete his MBA. After that he would cut his business teeth working with his father in import/export, then look for a position with a major corporation. He also had a vague notion that his film and television minor at USC might help him land a producing job in Hollywood, given that he had already had some success in this area. (He had helped put himself through college by shooting Super Eight surf films and road-showing them up and down the California Coast at a buck a ticket, and both Rock Me On The Water and Regression Session had won good reviews.)

Nothing in McKnight's background pointed towards a career such as the one Jeff was holding out to him, yet everything in his soul told him that this was the right move to make. And as they talked it through at Jeff's home in Pupukea (the one blissfully unaware that the other was slowly detoxing from serious heroin addiction) they joked that here was a marriage made in heaven – Jeff knew all there was to know about surfing, Bob knew all there was to know about business, watch out surf industry!

Says McKnight: "At that stage Jeff was the one with the vision. He could see how big the whole thing could become, although I'm sure he never envisaged that it would grow to the size it is today. But he just knew it was a good product. Then when I started wearing Quiksilver trunks, I saw it too. It was like a bucket seat in a sports car. They just felt right, and no trunks in the United States felt like that. Everyone else was making swimwear, these were boardshorts."

Jeff had a few samples, a few fragments of industry advice from people like Alan Green and Duke Boyd, and some pretty good contacts around the surf shops from his days promoting Bing and Plastic Fantastic. But that was about it. Neither of them knew how to make surf trunks, nor did they know anyone who did. They decided to wing it, and while Jeff made plans for his move back to California, McKnight flew home to his parents.

McKnight Sr had mellowed somewhat by now, and helped Bob put a business plan together and track down some capital investment. The two partners had no idea how much start-up capital they would need, so McKnight thought of a large number and it was thirty thousand dollars. Two of his father's associates, Jim Kleeman and Steve Beasley agreed to put up fifteen thousand apiece for a thirty per cent stake in the new company.

When Jeff arrived he set up home at Cindy's parents' place in Long Beach, and McKnight would drive up each morning in his campervan to start the business of the day. Says McKnight: "Mostly it was just driving around. We'd drive up to LA and try to source some fabric, then we'd drive out to Santa Ana to find a cutter, then we'd drive down to Encinitas and find someone who could assemble the shorts. We were making it up as we went along, and it was really hard work. In fact I'm sure this was the hardest Jeff had ever worked in his life, but he was great at it. He'd think things through and come up with solutions. One day I went to pick him up and Cindy came to the door. She said, 'You gotta see this. He's been like it all night.' We tiptoed into the bedroom and Jeff's lying on the bed with his eyes wide open, opening and closing a Velcro fly. He was working through one of our problems and he was oblivious to everything else."

When Jeff ate the doily in Torquay and won the American licence, he got a firm handshake and very little else, Alan Green being basically of the opinion that the new boys would have to do what he and John Law had done, which was start from the very beginning. He did, however, put them in touch with Walter Hoffman, one of the pioneers of the surf trunk game.

McKnight recalls: "Walter told us we were out of our friggin' minds. He said we should plan on losing all our money. But then he kind of softened and started to put us onto the right people. He said, 'The first thing you gotta do is go to New York and learn about fabric. You learn how to buy the best, then you pay for it on time until you got A-plus credit. Then you're serious, then you might make some money.' So I did what he said, I went to New York in the middle of winter, snow on the ground, and I walked the beat and made the contacts. They asked me how much fabric I wanted to buy and I didn't even know. I said, I don't know, enough to make a couple hundred pairs! God, we were dumb!"

Through his New York contacts, McKnight was able to source fabric through a "jobber" in Los Angeles, but only in disgusting gold and bisque. He and Jeff had three hundred pairs made up, with McKnight putting the snaps in and Jeff ironing them in Bob's parents' garage. They had three surf shop clients – Hobie Surfboards at Dana Point, Newport Surf and Sport and Val Surf in the San Fernando Valley.

Quiksilvers had been dribbling into California as imports for a couple of years and had established some recognition in the market, but more importantly they had an "as worn by the stars" quality which had come about not through clever recruiting of high profile surfers, but simply because the best surfers insisted on wearing them. On the cover of the May 1976 edition of *Surfing* magazine, for example, Mark Richards was shown tucking into a tube at Off The Wall, the Lightning Bolt logo on his surfboard and the Quiksilver logo on his shorts clearly visible. The magazine's centrespread also featured Richards in his Quiksilvers.

Says Alan Green: "This was still pretty much the early days of international travel as far as most surfers were concerned. They didn't get around the way they do today, and the Quiksilver label was identified with a kind of worldliness, like you knew what was happening out there in the frontline."

The same thing had happened a generation earlier, when Californian surfers started returning from their Hawaiian sojourns with trunks made first by Take in Waikiki, then by M. Nii, in his little tailor shop in Waianae. A pair of M. Niis showed the world you'd surfed Hawaii. Twenty years later a pair of Quiksilvers showed the world you were a serious surfer.

Two weeks before the delivery of the first Quiksilver USA range, the Hobie shop at Dana Point put up a sign out on Pacific Coast Highway. It read, "Quiksilvers Coming Soon!" When they got their one hundred pairs, they changed it to, "They're Here!" And they sold out in three days.

Steve Pezman, then the publisher of *Surfer* magazine and always a keen student of surf sociology, believes that the arrival of Quiksilver signalled the end of an era. He says, with only a hint of a smirk: "All of California's surfing heritage was symbolised by the M. Nii trunk, which Hang Ten had adapted to make the classic California surf trunk. When Jeff Hakman brought over the yoke trunk, he did so at a time when a heavy Australian influence was being felt throughout our surfing culture. So, at the same time Californians started wearing Quiksilvers, they also stopped using words like gremlin and started saying grommet. Our sense of self began to dissolve very quickly."

But Jeff and McKnight's sense of self was on the upswing. Thrilled at their immediate success, the partners put together a regular production team of subcontractors, and set about opening accounts between San Diego and Santa Barbara. Every cent they made from the sale of each tiny range went straight back into the production of the rest, but they were building up their sales base at a rapid rate and the future looked positively rosy.

And three months into that first long and difficult summer, Jeff was as clean as a whistle. Once again, the flirtation with heroin seemed like someone else's nightmare. Could that really have been him? It seemed unthinkable.

CHAPTER 26

In early November 1976, Jeff and Bob McKnight were sitting around in their new factory (a basic industrial shed) in Seventeenth Street in Costa Mesa, just behind Newport Beach. Inside the factory they had virtually nothing except a long bench with their shorts stacked in neat piles in varying sizes. It was late afternoon, they had been working too hard and they were about ready for a beer. But first, they were in deep and pleasurable contemplation of both the quality and quantity of their range, which had grown considerably from their first run of three hundred garments.

The phone rang and McKnight heard his partner say: "Greenie! You're where? Bullshit! No kidding? We'll be right down."

Alan Green had phoned from a nearby restaurant. "Come on, Buzz," said Jeff, "Time for you to meet our founder". He didn't mention that Green was as drunk as a skunk.

It says a lot for the state of the protagonists in the story which is about to unfold, but none of them can agree on where it began. Some say Chuck's Steakhouse, others insist it was the Charthouse. Alan Green says it was definitely "The Woman With No Head". (He means The Quiet Woman in Newport.) But wherever it was, Jeff and McKnight walked in stone cold sober and found Green propped up in a booth, surrounded by empty wine bottles. With him were Paul Neilsen, journalist turned film-maker Harry Hodge and Torquay surfer Dick Alcott. Clearly the binge had been in progress for several hours and they were all talking gibberish.

Says Bob McKnight: "I didn't know what to make of this crew, but an hour later we're all in a black Lincoln Continental hauling ass to Vegas. Three in the front, three in the back, beers, tequilas, cigarettes, bad jokes and fast driving."

Says Alan Green: "I think we were trying to break the record for driving from the coast to Vegas. Something like that. There were no speed limits and the drink driving laws weren't as stringent as they are now, and we were just going for it. Neilsen was driving and he hit a fifteen miles per hour exit ramp doing ninety! He wasn't game to turn the wheel so we

Bruce Raymond, Paul Neilsen and Jeff at The Ranch, 1976.

Above: *Bob McKnight and Jeff with blondes, Florida trade show, 1977.*

Below: *Left to right, Jeff, Pete Wilson and Bob McKnight at Katin's contest, 1977.*

just sailed into space and arrived at this garage through the backyard. We yelled at the guy to fill her up and all bolted for the toilet. At one stage Jeff was driving but we reckoned he was going too slowly, so we just pulled him right out of the driver's seat and replaced him with Paul without missing a beat. We were trying to get the car to surf, you know, chucking re-entries and lip bashes off the edge of the tarmac. About ten miles out we saw the lights of Vegas dead ahead but the road veered left. We just kept going straight on, bashing over all the cactus in our path. We made it almost into town before we had to get back on the road."

Says Paul Neilsen: "We had to average ninety miles an hour to break the existing speed record. When you're drinking a lot of beer you've got to allow for piss stops, so that meant I had to keep the needle around one hundred and five. It was just fucking mad!"

When the mists of the hangovers had cleared and they had lost enough money to make it all worthwhile, the naughty boys headed back to Orange County and the real purpose of Alan Green's visit.

Says Jeff: "He was checking us out. He didn't say much, but I think he was horrified by our business act. I mean. we really didn't have one. We were trying but we had a long way to go. He was probably disgusted, but he tried not to show it. He tried to just set us straight."

Alan Green recalls: "Hakman and McKnight simply didn't know anything about the industry. They probably had a bit of an idea about how to sell boardshorts, but they didn't know how to build them, so I spent quite a bit of time helping Bob with the technical side of it. But I wasn't worried about them having the licence. They were good, honest blokes, they were sincere and they were prepared to have a go. What more could you want? McKnight had an MBA but he didn't act like it. He just seemed normal to me."

By December the partners had their orders in for next summer and it looked like they would turn over sixty thousand dollars in their first year of trading. It wasn't quite a business, but it was a start. Bob suggested Jeff head back to Hawaii for a few weeks. He had been invited to the Duke meet and, despite his protestations that he had given up professional surfing, Bob felt his appearance would be good for business. But Jeff had a disastrous contest, breaking a board at Sunset in the preliminaries and failing to advance. Enough was enough. At twenty-eight years of age, he officially retired.

Australia's Peter Townend was named world professional champion that year by the International Professional Surfers (IPS) tour, signalling the beginning of a truly global tour, at which Jeff would never have excelled. It was Townend, an avid statistician, who in February 1980 compiled a statistical report for *Surfing* magazine on pro surfing in the 1970s. The statistics clearly showed Jeff Hakman's place in the history of the sport. Although he competed in only a handful of events in the IPS era, during which prize money escalated dramatically, Jeff was rated the seventh highest money winner for the decade, he was rated equal third for number of victories in the decade even though he only competed for six years of it, and in the 1976 IPS ratings he finished ninth, despite the fact that he only competed in three events.

In a 70s retrospective article in the same special issue of *Surfing*, surfer/journalist Michael Tomson said of Jeff: "Throughout the late sixties and early seventies Jeff Hakman was the most successful total surfer. He dominated competition in Hawaii for nearly eight years until the Australian takeover in 1975."

Well, it had been good, real good, but it was over. Jeff put his Pupukea house on the market and flew back to the factory.

Accounts were growing faster than profits and Quiksilver USA needed more working capital to fund the summer range, so Jeff and McKnight went back to their silent partners and asked for more money. Not surprisingly, they wanted more stock, but both Jeff and Bob were becoming disillusioned by their cold appraisal of the business. They weren't surfers, they just didn't understand.

McKnight's college buddy Peter Wilson was standing by, and he said his father was prepared to put up his investment portfolio to guarantee a line of credit. With Jeff and Bob's approval, Wilson bought out Kleeman and Beasley and helped Quiksilver get access to the kind of money it needed to grow. Says McKnight: "That injection of funds was what really got us started. By the summer of 1977, we were a real business."

Harry Hodge rolled through Newport Beach that summer, filming for his surf epic Band On The Run, an ambitious attempt to recreate Bruce Brown's classic surf travelogue, The Endless Summer, with Hollywood production values. Hodge had with him his surfing cast of Rabbit Bartholomew, Paul Neilsen, Bruce Raymond and Brian Cregan. In California they linked up with Jeff for a surfing and filming trip to The Ranch, and also shot footage of Jeff at work at Quiksilver.

The segment pictures Jeff as a happy and successful surfer-businessman, working at something he loves. Sadly, nothing could have been further from the truth. With new money in the company, he and McKnight had started to pay each other a small salary, and Jeff and Cindy had moved out of her parents' home and into a small apartment in Newport Beach. Jeff was trying to focus on the business but it wasn't making him happy, and as Pete Wilson became involved, he felt himself being pushed out of a meaningful role.

But Jeff's dissatisfaction went deeper than that. Basically, he'd been away from California for too long. He felt like a fish out of water, and his solution to the problem was to seek out his old friend heroin. Jeff knew a connection in Newport Beach, and he and Cindy started weekend dabbling. By midsummer it was every night dabbling at a level they could not afford, but then the Pupukea house sold and Jeff had twenty thousand dollars in his pocket, briefly.

Jeff recalls: "A normal person would have been really happy with the situation – the business was firing, I had good friends and business partners – but I wasn't, and I used heroin to make me happy. It seemed okay to do that because this was California in the late 1970s and everyone I knew was into drugs. It was just all over the place and I fell into it very easily because I felt trapped in my life. Both Bob and Pete had grown up in California, all their friends were there, their lives revolved around the place. The only life I felt comfortable with there was the one I shared with my nocturnal friends, and I drifted more and more towards their scene."

In 1978 Jeff and Cindy drifted apart. Says Jeff: "We were really comfortable together, we didn't fight and we seemed to enjoy the same things, like heroin. But there was something missing there, and I guess it was love."

Jeff moved out of the apartment and Cindy moved back to her parents' home at Long Beach. The split triggered a drug binge that lasted right through the summer. Jeff had a salary and the remains of the proceeds from the sale of the Pupukea house, so he had just enough money to get into trouble, and he found himself making excuses at work each day to drive down to San Juan Capistrano, where both Surfer and Surfing magazines had their offices. Most times he wouldn't get that far. The dealer of the day lived at Laguna Beach and Jeff would drop by and pick up a quarter gram of heroin for one hundred and fifty dollars, or sometimes a half for two hundred and fifty. The dealer obligingly showed him how to make his drugs go further.

"The guy was into shooting and so I tried it. I'd long gone past the stage where that would have repulsed me. It was a good rush and it made your stuff last twice as long, so I got into it. Pretty soon I was shooting heroin and cocaine into my veins every day, and the only time I'd let up and go back to smoking or snorting it was when the tracks on my arms got too obvious. I found the mixture of heroin and cocaine a very seductive thing. You'd shoot a speedball and there'd be this totally euphoric rush. One night I sat in a room with a Hawaiian surfer and we shot speedballs all night. Every twenty minutes, wham! In the morning my head had blown up into this huge balloon. It was so scary I had to go to a doctor. I told him what I'd been doing and he said I was lucky to be alive. But he gave me something to relieve the swelling and I went right back to my speedballs."

FLAME

The Ranch, 1976.

FLAME

Eventually, Jeff said: "Is there anything I can do to save my job? I love you guys, I love the company. I don't want to go, but I understand completely if you want me to."

Winship was disposed to give him another chance. Brigitte was hard line. She had strong views about ethics in business and in her mind, Jeff had crossed the line and there was no stepping back. Interviewed for this book almost ten years later, she had softened in her view of Jeff as a person, but she still regarded the incident as the most distressing in the company's history.

So it was down to Harry to make the casting vote. He says now it was the toughest call he has had to make in business. He said then: "Jeff, I want you to sign a letter of resignation. I'm going to keep it in my office safe, and if there is any problem in the future, you're out. No notice, no warnings. Out. I want Cherie as a signatory on all your bank accounts and credit cards, and I want you to do something about yourself. You have to do something about yourself. You're not a fucking kid any more, Jeff. You're killing yourself and you're killing us."

Jeff recalls: "I wish I could explain how bad I felt, how incredibly guilty I felt that I had let down my friends again. But at that time I didn't know what I know now about drugs and about myself. This thing would just wash over me like a huge wave, and I had no answer to it. I didn't know how to duck-dive."

The shocking reality of his addiction underlined everything Jeff did in the coming months, and he threw everything into his work to keep from falling into an abyss of depression and self pity. Fortunately he had a specific project. Quiksilver Europe had embarked upon its most expensive and most audacious image marketing campaign, sponsoring the 1986 amateur world surfing championships at Newquay on the Cornish coast of England.

Billed as "the world's largest surfing contest", the Quiksilver World Titles featured teams from sixteen countries, including first timers Sweden, Norway and Holland. The French entered two teams, one from France itself, the other from her colonial outposts like Tahiti and the Reunion Islands, while Spain, Great Britain and Ireland completed the European presence. Never before had the world contest been hosted by Britain, and the inclusion of so many teams from Europe guaranteed massive press coverage throughout Quiksilver's market. The project cost the company more than one hundred thousand US dollars, but the benefit from creating a brand awareness in markets outside the surfing "core" was worth ten times that amount.

As contest director, Jeff spent months battling the logistics, organising locations and creating a workable format for the event. For a junkie fraudster in remission, it was a welcome distraction.

Above: *Jeff, Harry and Bruce at Jeff's 40th in Biarritz.*

Right: *Jeff and Phil Grace, last car to Pamplona.*

Opposite: *Jeff, Cherie, Harry and Sandee – early days in the mountains, Verbier, 1987.*

R S BECK

Above and opposite: Quiksilver World Amateur Championships,
Newquay, UK, 1986.

Jeff snowboarding in France.

That fall and winter he was presented with another distraction in the form of the new sport of snowboarding. Quiksilver had already tackled the mountains, but this exciting new sport, which combined elements of surfing and skiing with an aggressive, youthful arrogance, gave the company the perfect vehicle to go big time into winter sportswear. Much as they had done all over Europe a couple of years earlier, Harry and Jeff went off on a "look and listen" mission. They spent endless days on the mountain, developing an understanding of the sport and its homey young gurus, and when they went back to their design team, they knew exactly what would sell.

Sometimes in these years it seemed to Jeff that compassion and understanding was pretty much a one-way street. Whenever he really needed either, someone was there to provide it. There were pricks and charlatans in his life who would use him up and work him over and hand him the needle to finish him off, but there were also people who were always there to pick him up, dust him off, and help him start again. He tended to forget why those people stuck by him, why they felt he was worth the effort. Harry Hodge knew why.

By the end of 1986 Harry's relationship with Brigitte was over and he had entered a phase in his life that his friends now refer to as "the ugly bachelor period". He was hitting the bars around Biarritz on a nightly basis. Often he would phone Jeff at home and order him to a "business meeting" at the Carlos Bar on the Cote des Basques. The main item on the agenda was getting drunk, but this didn't help Jeff's home life, particularly when Cherie had just put dinner on the table.

Jeff kept his own counsel on this until one night Harry left the Bodega Beau Rivage (the old Biarritz Steakhouse), took off at a great rate and spun out on the wet street, bringing a light pole down as he crashed into the kerb. Stunned, but otherwise unhurt, he picked up his briefcase and walked back to the bar. Quiksilver executive Jeff Bradburn was still there. He looked surprised to see his boss back so soon. Hodge pointed out the window at the steaming wreck and the police and fire engines surrounding it.

"Oh shit!" said Bradburn.

Top left: *The Hakmans in Tahiti.*
Left and above: *Ryan Hakman, budding surf star.*

The former rugby star from New Zealand was well connected in Biarritz and he immediately took Harry back to the scene to show the police that the driver had survived. The gendarmes took one look at Harry and told Bradburn to get his friend the hell out of there or they'd have to arrest him. Hodge, whose French wasn't up to much at this stage, even when sober, thought they were telling him he was under arrest, and obligingly climbed into the back of the police Citroen and sat on the gendarme's hat.

Harry had to fly to Australia the next day, leaving the messy aftermath of his binge for others to clean up. But when he got back, Jeff took him aside immediately. He said: "Harry, this might sound weird coming from me, but you have a little bit of a problem. You know when you go into a bar sometimes, and there'll be this guy, around forty, drunk, trying to hustle young chicks, trying to act about twenty-five. He's ugly, Harry. He's the ugly bachelor, and in a couple of years, that's you."

Harry took the advice as it was intended, but the problem had already been solved. In Sydney he had met Sandee Jonsen and fallen in love. Within a couple of months she had joined him in France, and within a year she was Mrs Harry Hodge.

In 1988 Jeff and Cherie decided it was time they tied the knot too. They were married in front of family and friends at the Mirage Resort on the Gold Coast of Queensland.

The quality of life had improved greatly for the Hakman family, but Cherie still lived in fear that one day Jeff would succumb to the old demons and they would lose everything again. She had become close friends with Sandee Hodge, and confided in her. At the instigation of the two wives, Harry did some research into drug rehabilitation programs in different parts of the world and discovered Galsworthy Lodge in central London. It seemed to offer a long-term battle plan against addiction, rather than some overnight miracle cure, and Jeff agreed to give it a try. He flew to London and checked in for six weeks, sharing facilities with detoxifying alcoholics and drug addicts of all persuasions.

He says: "The very first thing I had to come to terms with was the acceptance of a higher power, a spiritual entity to whom you can turn over your own will. Fortunately, I'd always believed that life was too good for us to have invented, that there had to be something bigger. So I was able to do that. I came to understand that addiction means you have no control over this thing unless you submit your will and learn to follow simple daily patterns. The philosophy was basically the twelve steps of Alcoholics Anonymous, but the therapy I found very, very powerful. It changed my self perception in every possible way."

When the program was over Jeff came home and was offered heroin almost immediately. For the first time since 1975, he was able to say no.

Above: Biarritz Surf Festival, 1993. Jeff, Nat Young, Toni and Gerry Lopez.

Right: Harry and Sandee's wedding.

The women in Jeff's life.
With Cherie and Doris at Jeff and Cherie's wedding, Gold Coast, 1988.

171

CHAPTER 32

The signing. Left to right, Brigitte Darrigrand, Jeff, John Winship, Harry, Randy Herrel.

In 1986 Quiksilver USA became the first surf industry company to go on the stock market. The float gave them enough capital to look for investments, and in early 1990 they decided take a close look at Quiksilver Na Pali.

Harry Hodge had been devoting more and more time and energy to babysitting the French banks who had allowed the company overdraft to blow out with the sales growth and were understandably edgy. Hodge knew that if Na Pali was to achieve its full potential in Europe the company would have to shore up its fiscal security with new money, so he began to scour the financial capitals and tax havens of Europe looking for investment capital.

Hodge found plenty of interested investors, but their money always came at a price he couldn't afford. The would-be backers wanted to turn Quiksilver into anything but what it was good at, from hang glider production to industrial clothing. They couldn't see the surfboards for the trees. Internationally, Quiksilver had positioned itself as the global leader in its field through strict adherence to what it liked to refer to as "core" products and marketing strategies. Bruce Raymond, the international director of Quiksilver, liked to remind licensees around the world that Quiksilver is and always was "a boardriding company", referring to the boards used in surfing, windsurfing, snowboarding and skateboarding. The image cleverly covered these fast-growing extreme sports in every geographical situation in every major population centre on earth.

The surf industry was littered with the corpses of companies that had strayed too far from their roots, and men like Raymond, Green, Law, McKnight, Hakman and Hodge well knew it. So when McKnight and his then-chief executive John Warner approached Na Pali as possible investors, Hodge was very happy to discuss all the possibilities. For McKnight and Warner, however, there was only one possibility. They wanted to buy one hundred per cent of the company.

As the negotiations proceeded it became obvious to Hodge and his partners that the

Above: Jeff and Ryan at Waimea Bay in December 1993, remembering Eddie Aikau.

Left: Cherie and Jeff at Courchevel, 1995.

Fun at Hanalei Bay.
Above: *Jeff at Pine Trees.*

Opposite page: *Ryan, sittin' and waitin'. The kid can surf!*

proposition on the table was too good to pass up. However there were major problems with this for Quiksilver International. Hodge had kept Green, Raymond and Law informed at every stage, but as a deal seemed more likely, they began to closely examine the global impact on the label. A merger or internal buyout of this magnitude meant that the licensing company would have to look very closely at its own corporate operations. On the other hand, it meant that Quiksilver would be unshakeable in all its major markets. The directors took in the big picture and decided to support the deal.

Quiksilver Europe was, and still is, a remarkable success story. From the very beginning right through to the merger deal, Jeff and Harry got plenty of support from mentors and friends like Alan Green, John Law, Bruce Raymond and Bob McKnight. But in many ways the pupils had become the teachers, and today Quiksilver Na Pali is the most successful and profitable Quiksilver licensee in the world. At the time of the merger talks its turnover had grown twenty-six-fold in just six years (from one million US dollars to twenty six million) and by 1996 this had grown to seventy two million dollars. In addition to this staggering growth, the company had introduced globally such innovations as snow products, a women's division and the Quiksilver Boardriders Clubs franchise. But the statistic Harry and Jeff were most proud of was that they had achieved all this without betraying the label's roots. Where other surf labels had gone running to the mainstream for financial security, Quiksilver did less than three per cent of its business with department stores.

Jeff, Harry, John and Brigitte walked out of the deal-signing as multi-millionaires, but more importantly, they were still charged with the responsibility of running the company. However the partnership would never be the same again. The very nature of what Quiksilver Inc liked to refer to as a "merger" meant that Harry Hodge would be propelled into a higher profile as chief executive of Na Pali, while the others would have to redefine their roles. In the months and years ahead, this is precisely what happened.

John Winship "retired", while Brigitte Darrigrand remained involved in human resource management.

Jeff moved back into his natural marketing role, with a free and easy brief to get out into the marketplace and bring back the knowledge. He remained restless however, and in 1993 he and Cherie decided they had had enough of living in France full time. He offered to quit the company, but Harry, reaalising the importance of his position as one of surfing's leading icons, proposed a more flexible arrangement that meant Jeff would continue his important role in marketing, retain his international association with Quiksilver, while dividing his time between France and Australia.

The Hakmans, now with baby Lea, born in October 1993, moved firstly to Coffs Harbour on the New South Wales north coast, near Cherie's parents and sisters. Jeff felt quite comfortable there but Cherie hated it. They moved again, this time to Noosa Heads in Queensland. Jeff liked the village atmosphere, but there was surf only three or four months of the year and the rest of the time people sat in cafes in designer gear and sipped cafe lattes.

During the Hawaiian winter of 1993, Jeff returned to the North Shore for a Quiksilver conference. He surfed Sunset again for the first time in more than a decade, felt the tingle of the trade winds on his back and the thrill of the glide in his gut. He was home.

After the conference he flew to Kauai and looked at real estate. A few months later the Hakmans bought a comfortable home in Princeville, directly above Hanalei Bay.

When I visited Jeff on Kauai in May 1996, to begin work on this book, we cruised around the old hippie town in his pickup, surfed the little beach breaks at Pine Trees on longboards and drank sunset beers looking out over the most beautiful valley on earth.

Jeff Hakman was in his element. At forty-seven years of age he was a happy man with a loving wife and two beautiful children. A lucky man.

And living one day at a time.

Jeff, G-land, 1996.

EPILOGUE by Harry Hodge

In 1993 Quiksilver scheduled its annual international meeting on the North Shore of Oahu at a rented house at Sunset Beach, with Jeff Hakman attending for the first time since his departure from Quiksilver USA in 1983.

Since his demise at Newport Beach he had always felt awkward and uncomfortable in the presence of the people he felt he had let down so badly, and they would all be gathered here together. Understandably, Jeff approached the meetings with trepidation.

He arrived a week early and spent the time surfing clean six feet waves at Pupukea on a longboard. He was in great shape for a forty-four-year-old, and by week's end he felt at ease with the power of the North Shore, if not with the events to come.

When Jeff picked me up at Honolulu Airport I could tell he was nervous, and we talked about it as we drove out to the North Shore. We discussed how the best way to gain respect from the people who mattered in the company, was to do it out on the water. That was where it had all started, and that was where it should end.

The next day Sunset was on the way up with ten feet waves predicted by late afternoon. Jeff had been awaiting the arrival of a new seven feet eight inch board that Maurice Cole had shaped him in France, and we drove over to shaper Pat Rawson's place to pick it up. When the protective cardboard and bubble-wrap had been removed, Jeff began a ceremony I have seen many times over the years. He picked the board up under his right arm, then looked along the rail to the nose, then back to the tail. He then put the board on the ground, stepped back behind the tail and stared. Next he picked it up by the tail and looked at the bottom. Then he put it back under his right arm and started again.

Having seen him go through this ritual often, I could tell that the board was one he could not relate to. The last time he had surfed Sunset, ten years earlier, boards were different. They might have progressed, but his mindset about this special place had not.

Jeff strapped the board on the roof and we started to drive to Sunset, but then he changed his mind and suggested we stop at Mike Miller's house at Pupukea. He said Mike had plenty of boards in his garage, and maybe he'd just look them over.

At Miller's we opened the garage door and saw about fifty boards on racks. Jeff pulled out a yellow Brewer. I thought, what else? And he began his ceremony all over again. The board had more thickness and length and Jeff said he felt more comfortable with it. I guessed that it had to be ten years old, maybe more, but all of Miller's boards were in immaculate condition.

Back at Sunset he waxed up on the lawn of the rented house and then watched the surf for fifteen minutes. Finally he picked up the Brewer and paddled out over Val's Reef into the channel. The late afternoon light made vision difficult, but I went inside the house and watched through binoculars. I could recognise several of the current top surfers out in the lineup, then I saw Jeff knee-paddling (the only surfer on his knees) towards them. I watched a couple of sets come through and some of the top pros took off and got good rides. But not Jeff.

Then a large set loomed on the horizon. I focused on the biggest wave of the set and watched a lone surfer deep inside and paddling into a solid ten feet west peak. As soon as he stood up I knew it was Jeff Hakman. He slid effortlessly to the bottom and hooked one of his trademark bottom turns, then wound high into the feathering peak. Then he straight-lined down the face again for his next bottom turn and back high into the inside wall. Nothing vertical and radical like today's hotshots, but a typically, controlled and measured ride. He kicked out in front of a few paddlers, dropped to his knees and headed back out to the lineup.

I took the binoculars away and realised I had tears streaming down my face. I quickly looked around, embarrassed that some one might have been watching me watching Jeff.

G-land, 1996.
Above: *Jeff recovers from a head wound.*

There was no one, so I let the emotion flow out of me. I knew I'd seen Jeff's first Sunset wave in fifteen years, and probably his best in twenty. After all we'd been through together, I thought it only just that I should share that moment.

Jeff surfed until dark with his Quiksilver buddies Bruce Raymond, Bob McKnight and John Law. Our meetings went like a dream, and Jeff showed none of the awkwardness of the past. No one said a word, but I knew that there was a general relief in the camp. Hakman was back, and he'd made his point with deeds, not words.

That was always Jeff's real style.

BERNARD TESTEMALE

179

SCENES FROM A LIFE

ERIC CHAUCHE

ERIC CHAUCHE

Scenes from the Biarritz Surf Festival in 1993, a celebration of surfing's roots and a bonding between the surfing communities of Hawaii and France.

ERIC CHAUCHE3

Above: Wayne Lynch, Gerry Lopez and Jeff.
Below: Jeff with Buffalo Keaulana.

ERIC CHAUCHE

Wherever he has lived, Jeff has maintained his close ties with the Hawaiian people.

Left: With George Downing.

Below: Jeff and Cherie at the opening ceremony for the Quiksilver In Memory Of Eddie Aikau.

ERIC CHAUCHE

ERIC CHAUCHE

Above: *Jeff and Ryan with Reynolds Wright.*
Left: *Jeff with Rusty Keaulana.*

Surfing has always been the thread that holds Jeff's life together. He particularly loves the thrill of surfing lonely spots with close friends.

Above: With Maritxu Darrigrand at Hanalei Bay.

Right: Canary Islands secret spot.

Below: Morocco.

Opposite: Guethary.

ERIC CHAUCHE

ERIC CHAUCHE

PETER WILSON

ERIC CHAUCHÉ

Top: Tom Carroll signs the first $1 million sponsorship deal, Jeff looks on.

Above: Dressed for work.

Left: Quiksilver Europe's 10th anniversary.

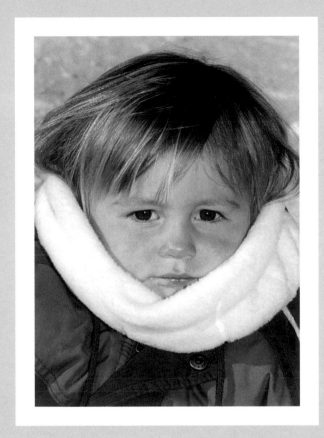

Top left: *Lea Hakman.*
Above: *Cherie and Jeff, France 1996.*
Left: *Jeff and Ryan 1996.*

JEFF HORNBAKER

Left: 1996 portrait of Jeff at Cote des Basques.
Below: Jeff with Harry and Sandee.

KELLY SLATER

CATCHING UP

Nat Young at Honolua Bay, 1967.

Reno Abellira
Now lives in Santa Monica, California. Shapes a few surfboards.

Eddie and Clyde Aikau
Eddie died tragically and heroically in 1978, paddling for help during the ceremonial voyage of the Hokulea, between Hawaii and Tahiti. Clyde runs a beach concession for a major hotel at Diamond Head.

Jose Angel
Jose died in a diving accident in the 1980s.

Butch Van Artsdalen
Dropped out of surfing and died young of liver disease.

Duke Boyd
Now lives in San Juan Capistrano, California, where he is developing a new clothing line.

Dick Brewer
Still shaping surfboards on Kauai. Still the master craftsman after four decades. Quiksilver's Bruce Raymond organised a "guru tour" of Australia in which Brewer held his audiences of surfboard industry professionals spellbound.

Gary Chapman
Now living in San Clemente, California. In 1996 Gary had a leg amputated, but plans to start surfing with an artificial limb in 1997. In the history of surfing, his accomplishments have been monumental but sadly understated.

Gerry Lopez

JOHN WITZIG

Peter Cole
Still living at Rocky Point, Peter has been surfing big waves longer than anyone else on the planet!

Mickey Dora
Now in his sixties, Dora spends most of his time at Jeffrey's Bay, South Africa, surfing and being mysterious. He tries to make it up to Biarritz every year for a week or two of cultural enlightenment.

Fred Van Dyke
Living at Kailua on Oahu. Still surfing and in great shape, Fred tones up with regular hiking trips in Northern California.

Midget Farrelly
After many years of shunning all social contact with the sport he once dominated, a mellower Farrelly in his fifties is an occasional guest of honour at longboard meets.

Harry and Doris Hakman
Harry got bent and can't go diving for exotic fish as often as he would like these days, but he still pursues an active lifestyle near Makaha and dreams about sailing away in his yacht with his girlfriend Shiggy. Doris lives in a Honolulu apartment and is still mad about tennis. She travels the world competing in seniors tournaments, and, at 70, became the pro for all Pearl Harbour tennis facilities.

Jeannine and Laurie Hakman
Jeannine lives in Honolulu with her two daughters. Laurie and her family live in Santa Cruz, California.

Bill Hamilton
Lives on Kauai with his girlfriend, shapes state of the art surfboards and surfs every day he can.

Fred Hemmings
Having failed in his brave attempt to become lieutenant governor of Hawaii, Freddy is working as a consultant while planning his next political move. He still surfs, with great style, on a very big board.

Duke Kahanomoku
Duke passed away in 1967. The entire CBD of Waikiki shut down for his funeral. Jeff was one of the mourners. Although the Duke Classic has also passed into history, Duke is remembered always as the father of modern surfing.

Buddy Boy Kaohe
Died of an overdose of heroin.

Gerry Lopez
A convert to snowboarding, Gerry divides his time between homes in Bend, Oregon and Maui. A devoted husband and father, he still finds time for surfing adventures in exotic locations all over the world, and promotional work for a European-based clothing company.

Bob McTavish
Bob still lives a stone's throw from the lineup at Lennox Head on Australia's east coast, where he surfs whenever he can. A keen student of surfing history, he has lately taken to

building exquisite museum-piece surfboards and to writing about the evolution of surfboard design.

Mike Miller
Lives on a yacht, usually moored at an exotic location. Loves surfing, golf and privacy.

Paul Neilsen
Brothers Neilsen has become a highly successful chain of surf shops and Paul spends much of his time managing the business, but when Burleigh calls, he is one of the first to answer. A doting father, he has also become a leading light in surf coaching.

Greg Noll
Lives in Crescent City, Northern California with wife Laura. Makes the most authentic redwood and balsa collector surfboards in the world.

Jock Sutherland
Lives on the North Shore of Oahu. His son is as gifted as he was. Both surf all the time.

Greg Tucker
Died in a car crash in Central America some years ago.

Nat Young
Nat and his family live at Angourie, on the Australian east coast, where he is often seen in the lineup. His boutique hotel and apartments, Nat's At The Point, is a favourite of surfers and their families.

The Duke and Greg Noll with the Duke Kahanamoku Surf Team, 1966.

JEFF DIVINE

First published in 1997 by by Gen X Publishing, Park Place,
Canary Wharf, London, E144HJ, United Kingdom
in association with
General Publishing Group

Design and production by John Witzig & Company
Mullumbimby, NSW 2482, Australia

Printed in Singapore by Toppan Printing Co (Australia) Pty Ltd

Every effort has been made to find the photographers of the
many pictures that have come from personal collections. To those
whose work has not been credited, or may have been wrongly
attributed, the publishers offer an apology.

British Library Cataloguing in Publication Data
Jarratt, Phil
 Mr Sunset: the Jeff Hakman story
 1. Hakman, Jeff 2. Surfers – United States – Biography
 3. Surfing – United States
 I. Title
 797.3'2'092
ISBN 0 9529680 0 2

Library of Congress Cataloging-in-Publication Data
Jarratt, Phil.
 Mr. Sunset: the Jeff Hakman story/by Phil Jarratt.
   p.   cm.
   ISBN 1-57544-065-2
   1. Hakman, Jeff. 2. Surfers–United States–Biography.
I. Title
GV838.H35J37 1997
797.32'092–dc21
[B]   96-39935
                                           CIP